THE
Kids Care
BOOK

50 CLASS PROJECTS THAT HELP KIDS HELP OTHERS

By Joan Novelli and Beth Chayet

SCHOLASTIC
PROFESSIONAL BOOKS

New York • Toronto • London • Auckland • Sydney

To all kids who care

J.N. and B.C.

No part of this publication, with the exception of the Kids Care Contest entry form, may be reproduced in whole or in part, or stored in a retrieval system, or transmitted in any form or by any means, electronic, mechanical, photocopying, recording, or otherwise, without written permission of the publisher. For information regarding permission, write to Scholastic Inc., 730 Broadway, New York, NY, 10003

Cover Design by Vincent Ceci
Design and Illustration by Drew Hires

ISBN 0-590-49141-5

Copyright © 1991 by Scholastic Inc. All rights reserved.

1 2 3 4 5/9

Printed in the U.S.A.

Contents

5 INTRODUCTION

PEOPLE PARTNERSHIPS
Projects to improve people's lives—from befriending kindergartners just beginning school to helping immigrants prepare for the U.S. citizenship exam.

7 Adopt a Friend
9 Around the World
10 Food Goes Good
12 Head Start Helpers
14 Immigrant Aid
16 Journal Exchange
17 Neighborhood Friends
18 Read-Along Books for Pediatric Patients
19 TeleCare

COMMUNITY INVOLVEMENT
Projects to build a better community—from promoting traffic safety to restoring an historical landmark.

22 Adopt a Window
23 Bear Necessities
24 Bricks for Books
25 Fire Safety
26 Footsteps Into Our Past
28 Knowing the Facts
29 Making History
31 New Life for Books
32 Sharing School with Sick Kids
33 Stop, Look, Walk
34 Welcome to Our Community

SOCIAL ACTION
Projects to help solve the problems of hunger, homelessness, poverty, and drug abuse—from growing potatoes for people who don't have enough to eat to helping families build homes.

37 Crop Walk
38 Harvest for Hunger
40 Help Build a House
41 Keep Them Warm
42 Mayflower Card Company
44 Operation Brown Paper Bag
45 Quilt for the Community
47 Shops for Shelters
49 Stamp Out Drugs
50 Stone Soup

Continued

ENVIRONMENTAL ISSUES
Projects to clean up the air, land, and water—from encouraging the community, to compost, to testing for acid rain.

53 Coffee Cans for Composting
54 Earth Day Every Day
56 Energy Check
58 Monitoring the Rain
60 Operation Paint-the-Town
61 Rain Forest Breakfast
63 Salt Solutions
65 Saving the Earth

ANIMAL PROTECTION
Projects to protect animals—from organizing a pet-food drive for abused and unwanted animals to stopping the slaughter of dolphins.

68 Adopt a Sea Lion
69 Bird Buddies
71 Elephants Alive
73 Kids Give a Hoot
75 Letters for Marine Life
77 Pet Friends
79 Whale World

GLOBAL AWARENESS
Projects to increase awareness of the world as everyone's community—from promoting worldwide literacy to welcoming new immigrants.

82 Book Relief
84 Books for the World
86 Care Packages
88 Children to Children
89 Paper Cranes for Peace
91 Trees for Ireland

93 RESOURCES

95 ENTERING THE KIDS CARE CONTEST

INTRODUCTION

Every year, thousands of children across the country are showing their schools, communities, nation, and world that they care. They're teaching English to immigrants, rehabilitating injured wildlife, visiting sick children, collecting supplies for homeless shelters, teaming up with kids from other countries to promote cultural understanding, restoring historical landmarks, and more.

How can they do all this and go to school, too? More and more, teachers are making the subject of citizenship come alive in their classrooms with service projects such as those listed above. When students participate in service projects, they learn firsthand about the privileges and obligations of citizenship. And in participating in these projects, they're becoming active citizens, contributing to the success of their communities, nation, and world.

Service projects don't have to take time away from other subject areas. In fact, you'll find that many fit right into the subjects you're already teaching. Teacher Carolyn Rodgers advises, "Think of a service project not in terms of taking time out, but in terms of making it a part of your curriculum. It's not like adding something on, it's like expanding on what you already have. And it only enhances your students' education and their total responsibility to their community."

This book is designed to help you do that. It includes step-by-step directions for 50 projects—all of which have been successfully implemented by teachers and their students. Projects are organized by categories for easy reference. If your students are interested in adopting a whale, you'll find it in the Animal Protection chapter. If they have an elderly neighbor in need of assistance, you'll find a relevant project in People Partnerships. And if they want to encourage worldwide literacy, check out Global Awareness.

You'll find that most of the projects can be implemented by students in any grade. In some cases, slight modifications are all you'll need to tailor a project to your students.

Project descriptions include a *Project Goal*, identifying the point of the project; a *Project Summary*, to help you quickly grasp what the project involves; a *Citizenship Goal*, to help your students expand their understanding of citizenship; a *Preparation* section, to help you get ready; a *Procedure* section, to give you step-by-step directions; *Modifications*, suggesting options for adapting the project; and *Extension Activities*, to assist you in making curriculum connections.

You'll also find an annotated *Resources* section and information on planning and documenting your service project and entering it in the Kids Care Contest, a national contest sponsored by Scholastic News (Scholastic Inc.). All of the projects included in this book were Kids Care Contest entries. We offer a special thanks to all the teachers and kids who have participated in the Kids Care Contest—for sharing their projects with Scholastic News, for showing commitment to being caring citizens, and for inspiring this book.

Joan Novelli and Beth Chayet

1

People Partnerships

Projects to improve people's lives—from befriending kindergartners just beginning school to helping immigrants prepare for the U.S. citizenship exam.

Adopt a Friend

Around the World

Food Goes Good

Head-Start Helpers

Immigrant Aid

Journal Exchange

Neighborhood Friends

Read-Along Books for Pediatric Patients

TeleCare

Adopt a Friend

Project Goals
To make a difference in the life of a differently abled child and to educate others about disabilities and involve them in helping.

Project Summary
Laurie Beard's 1990–91 fourth-grade students at Orangefield Elementary School in Orangefield, Texas, "adopted" a child with cerebral palsy. They held a variety of fund-raisers to sponsor special activities with and for this child, including flying her home for Thanksgiving and Christmas. These students won a Kids Care Contest grand prize for their project.

Citizenship Goals
To realize that people working together can make a difference and motivate others to do the same; to recognize that despite differences, we all share certain needs and qualities.

Preparation
Contact a local center that works with children who have disabilities such as cerebral palsy. Ask for their assistance in teaming your students with a child who has a disability, such as cerebral palsy, and would benefit from a classroom of friends. Once your students have been teamed with a special pal, learn about this child's needs. For example, does he or she live away from home? If visits are possible, does the family need help financing them? When is your friend's birthday? What are some activities you could do together?

Procedure
1. Talk with your "adopted" friend about his or her special interests.
2. Bring parents and students together for an evening of brainstorming. Together, develop a list of projects and activities to sponsor, such as hand painting a T-shirt for your friend, signed by all of his or her new friends; celebrating his or her birthday; planting and caring for a garden; sending cards, letters, and artwork; visiting; and writing stories and keeping a photojournal about your activities.
3. Plan a schedule of activities, projects, and events.
4. Enjoy your new friend.

Modification
If it's not possible to set up personal visits with a child in a developmental center, share visits with one or more children at a center through videotapes. At different times throughout the year, help students tape special projects to share with these children. For example, have students choose, learn, and tell favorite stories for a storytelling

video. Have students rehearse jokes and take turns telling them for a comedy video.

Extension Activities

Language Arts: Initiate discussion in your class about differences among people using children's literature that deals with this issue. For example, *Let the Balloon Go* by Ivan Southall (Bradbury Press, 1968) tells the story of a 12-year-old boy who has cerebral palsy. "Like Me" by Emily Kingsley from *Free to Be a Family* by Marlo Thomas (Bantam, 1987) is a thought-provoking poem that will encourage students to look beyond differences.

Social Studies: Learn about laws that protect people with physical disabilities. Talk about how your school, businesses, and public places comply with access laws. What kinds of places make access difficult or impossible for people with physical handicaps? Brainstorm laws that would protect people with other kinds of disabilities.

Science: Have students invent a device that would solve a problem for a person with a disability. Have them identify the disability, isolate a problem, and invent and diagram a solution. If possible let students build models of their inventions.

Around the World

Project Goal
To learn about the culture of students from other countries.

Project Summary
Heidi Juran's 1988–89 third-grade students at Earle Johnson Elementary School in Golden, Colorado, teamed up with foreign students in their school. Each team made a book about that student and his or her country. They won a 1988–89 Kids Care Contest merit award for their project.

Citizenship Goal
To foster multicultural awareness among students.

Preparation
Team groups of students with foreign-born students in your school.

Procedure
1. Provide library time for groups to research and learn more about the other students' countries.
2. Have each group interview the student about his or her country and experiences in the United States.
3. Each group should make a chart showing similarities and differences between the United States and the country researched.
4. Have each group prepare a book featuring the foreign student. Display them in the library.

Modification
Team up with the children in your school who speak English as a second language. Invite them to read books with you. Schedule combined lunches with your ESL friends to provide a rich source of spontaneous language development. After lunch, play games together, sing songs, read big books, or just talk.

Extension Activities
Math/Social Studies: Follow recipes to prepare an international class lunch. Consult children's international cookbooks such as *Middle Eastern Food and Drink* by Christine Osborne (Bookwright, 1988) or *Cooking the Russian Way* by Gregory Plotkin and Rita Plotkin (Lerner, 1986).

Language Arts: Invite students featured in your books to teach your class some common words and phrases in their native languages, including words that students everywhere might use.

Modification Ideas from Leah Rukeyser's 1987–88 sixth-grade students at Columbus Elementary School, New Rochelle, New York (Kids Care Contest merit winners).

Food Goes Good

Project Goal
To help feed the homeless by coordinating efforts between homeless shelters and businesses.

Project Summary
Linda Strasburg's 1990–91 fifth-grade students at Inez Elementary Science and Technology Magnet School in Albuquerque, New Mexico, wrote letters to local delis, grocery stores, and bakeries asking them to donate their leftover food to homeless shelters instead of throwing it away. Students also wrote City Council members, the State Health Department, and a local food bank to find out if there were laws that prohibited business from donating unsold food. These students won a Kids Care Contest merit award for their project.

Citizenship Goals
To learn to help others less fortunate than themselves; to recognize difficulties in making changes involving many people and different value systems.

Preparation
Collect the names and addresses of delis, bakeries, and grocery stores in your community.

Procedure
1. Have students research whether or not there are laws in your city or state that prevent businesses from donating unsold food to the needy.
2. If no such laws exist, have students compose a letter to send to managers of local delis, stores, and bakeries informing them of your findings.
3. Take a trip to your local food bank to see how food is collected and distributed.
4. Arrange for volunteers (parents, teachers, and other community members) to pick up unsold food each day from businesses and take it to a homeless shelter, food bank, or soup kitchen.

Modification
Show a movie or put on a play about homelessness. Have admission to the play be nonperishable food items. Donate the food that is collected to a homeless shelter or food pantry.

Extension Activities
Language Arts: Help develop students' appreciation for their own homes. Read the poem "Home, You're Where It's Warm

Inside" by Jack Prelutsky from *The Random House Book of Poetry*, selected by Jack Prelutsky (Random House, 1983). Have students compose their own poems that describe what makes their homes special places.

Math: Ask local merchants to contribute to your campaign to help the homeless by accepting special coupons made by students. Have students make 5- or 10-cent coupons that can be used in the designated stores. Coupons should explain that the merchant will set aside the specified sum for the food bank or homeless shelter your class has selected. Be sure students list participating stores on the back of the coupons before distributing them to parents and community members. At the end of the month, have students collect the money from stores and tally the funds raised.

Social Studies: Designate a bulletin board for news related to homelessness. Encourage students to search magazines and newspapers for relevant articles. Discuss each article before posting it on the bulletin board. Some questions to talk about with students are: What are some of the reasons people may be homeless? What can you do to help the homeless? How would you feel if you and your family became homeless? What would you do to help your family?

Modification idea from Lois Wegner and her 1989–90 sixth- to eighth-grade students at Christ Child Academy, Sheboygan, Wisconsin.

Head Start Helpers

Project Goal
To support Head Start students in personal and academic growth.

Project Summary
Maria Prato's 1990–91 sixth-grade students at Spry Elementary School in Chicago, Illinois, teamed up with an area Head Start program to assist preschoolers in developing a range of skills. This class won a Kids Care Contest grand prize for its project.

Citizenship Goals
To develop and demonstrate care and concern for others and to model good citizenship for young children.

Preparation
Contact the site administrator of a local Head Start program to set up a partnership between your students and the preschoolers. Set up a schedule that will allow your students to meet with the preschoolers on a regular basis. For example, if the Head Start center is in or very near your school, you may be able to schedule your students to help out for half an hour every morning before their own classes start. If your entire class at once is too many helpers, set up a rotating schedule so that a different group of students goes in each morning of the week.

Procedure
1. Invite a Head Start instructor to meet with you and your students to discuss the goals of Head Start and the specific needs of the program's students. Together, develop a list of activities upper-grade students can work on with the preschoolers, such as:
• writing language experience stories—a preschooler tells a story while an upper-grade partner writes it down; afterwards, they can read the story together;
• practicing color identification, for example learning the color and word *blue* then having the preschoolers find everything in the room that is blue;
• learning safety signs in and out of the classroom;
• developing early math skills such as recognizing shapes and numbers;
• encouraging creativity through various visual and dramatic-arts activities;
• reinforcing good citizenship qualities, such as cooperation and respect for others, by modeling this in the classroom; and
• developing fine and gross motor skills by practicing tying shoes, buttoning shirts, playing catch and simple team games, and learning dances.
2. Schedule activities for each day students will be working at Head Start. For example, on Mondays, students might do language experience

stories about the weekend; on Tuesdays, students might lead so
and classifying activities, and so on.

3. Make the first day a get-to-know-each-other day. Play an ice-b
game—bring a Nerf ball, arrange everyone in a circle, and desig..
leader who starts the game by choosing a category such as names, says
his or her name, throws or rolls the ball to another person who gives his
or her name, and so on. Continue with other categories that will help everyone get to know one another, such as a favorite food, number of brothers and sisters, a wish, what you want to be when you grow up, and so on.

4. Continue with visits as scheduled.

Modification

Instead of adopting a younger class, team up with college freshmen and
sophomores who once attended your school. Students may be able to
suggest older brothers and sisters. Send them written messages of support. In return, your students are sure to develop growing enthusiasm
for their own education.

Extension Activities

Language Arts: Build Touch and Tell boxes to share with your young
partners to encourage vocabulary development of descriptive words.
Students can use empty shoe boxes or tissue boxes as containers and fill
them with a variety of items representing different textures. For example, a box filled with sandpaper, bark, a marble, a feather, and an un-
wrapped crayon can help the preschoolers learn descriptive words such
as *gritty*, *bumpy*, *slippery*, *silky*, and *waxy*.

Current Events: Have students read newspapers for news about education.
Set aside time each week to share the news. Discuss community or national issues in education as they arise. Have students write a class letter
to the editor of your newspaper expressing their opinions about an issue.

Citizenship: Turn your Kids Care project into a second Kids Care
Project to help your young partners develop their own citizenship
skills—work with them on a project within your project. For example, if
you're working with a preschool, kindergarten, or first-grade class, help
them set up a recycling project. If your state has a recycling law, set up
one bin in the classroom for collecting empty soda and juice cans and
another for collecting empty soda and juice bottles. Make arrangements
for returning the cans to a store for the deposit. Help students keep a
picture graph to show their progress. They can use the money they earn
to purchase books for their classroom.

*Modification Idea from Marilyn Lopez and her 1989-90 fourth-grade
students at T.L.R. Morgan Middle School, East Rochester, New York.*

Immigrant Aid

Project Goal
To help adult immigrants with the English language and help prepare them for the U.S. Citizenship Exam.

Project Summary
Roberta Jacoby's 1987–88 fourth-grade students at Myers Elementary School in Elkins Park, Pennsylvania, corresponded with adult immigrants and organized activities to help them acquire language skills and review U.S. historical facts in preparation for the citizenship exam. These students won a Kids Care Contest grand prize for their project.

Citizenship Goals
To appreciate the benefits of one's own citizenship and to help others gain access to the same.

Preparation
Contact local immigration organizations about your project. Ask them to team up your class with individuals who would like to participate. Invite an employee from an immigration and naturalization office to talk with students about what is involved in becoming a U.S. citizen.

Procedure
1. Begin corresponding with your pen pals. You may want to exchange both letters and audiotapes (if pen pals have access to a tape recorder). Because one of the goals is to help immigrants with the English language, it's important that students correspond in proper English (including spelling, in the case of letter writing).
2. Develop other techniques for teaching the English language. For example, create and perform a musical play that reviews English grammar, or make and share activity sheets that give practice in vocabulary skills, grammar, and so on.
3. Research historical information pertinent to the U.S. Citizenship Exam. Make illustrated flash cards that review this information. Invite your pen pals to school on a regular basis to review this information with students.

Modification
Welcome old and new immigrants to your city or town with a special breakfast. Plan to serve foods from each of the homelands represented. Post a large world map on the wall and invite your guests to show where they're from, talk about the customs in their native countries, and tell what they like about their new homes.

Extension Activities

Language Arts: Integrate multicultural studies with your curriculum by featuring children's literature from and about other countries and cultures in your classroom. Your school or local librarian can probably suggest some titles. A few to get you started are *Once There Were No Pandas* by Margaret Greaves (Dutton, 1985)—China; *What We've Brought You From Vietnam* by Phyllis Shalant (Messner, 1988)—Vietnam; *My Little Island* by Frane Lessac (HarperCollins, 1987)—Caribbean Islands; *I Am Eyes Ni Macho* by Leila Ward (Scholastic, 1987)—Kenya.

Social Studies: Invite foreign students in your school to take your class on imaginary trips to their countries. Display a large world map in your classroom; together locate your destination and use string to connect the countries you visit. Talk about how you can get there. Find out how long it takes to get there by all transportation options available. How much does each cost? What countries will you pass by, over, or through? Then make "passports" and *Bon Voyage!* Arrange to make and serve traditional dishes from each destination on your arrival days. Have your guest hosts talk about the climate, geography, things to do while you're visiting their countries, and so on.

Modification Idea from Heidi Juran and third-grade students, Earle Johnson Elementary School, Golden, Colorado; Kids Care Contest merit winner 1988–89.

Journal Exchange

Project Goal
To identify with, communicate with, and foster a sense of caring about elderly people.

Project Summary
Dorothy D'Arpino's 1988–89 second-grade students at L. W. Bills School in Herkimer, New York, teamed up with residents of a home for senior citizens and exchanged journals once a week. These students won a Kids Care Contest grand prize for their project.

Citizenship Goal
Students will learn about the needs of the elderly.

Preparation
Locate a nearby senior citizens' center interested in participating in this project. Explain the project and pair interested residents with individual students. Have students prepare a journal where they and their pen pals will write weekly entries to one another. Label each journal with both the student's and the pen pal's names.

Procedure
1. Each week students write in their journals to their pen pals. Their first note, for example, might tell something about themselves, what they are doing in school, or ask what kinds of things their pen pals did when they were in the same grade. Students may wish to include self-portraits or other drawings in their journals.
2. Deliver journals to the senior citizens' home so that students' pen pals can add their entries to the journals.
3. Pick up the journals as planned and return them to students for the next entry.
4. Repeat steps 1 through 3 weekly to maintain an ongoing correspondence between students and residents.

Modification
For elderly pen pals for whom writing is difficult, set up an oral journal using a cassette recorder to exchange entries. If your community does not have a nearby senior citizen home or center, set up a journal exchange with a veterans' home, a homeless shelter, or the children's wing or long-term patients' ward in a hospital.

Extension Activity
Art: Obtain a list of pen pals' birthdays. Assign a group of students to be responsible each month for designing, writing, and sending birthday wishes to residents with birthdays that month.

Neighborhood Friends

Project Goal
To provide on-going support to an elderly person or couple who needs assistance with routine and special activities.

Project Summary
Betsy Robinson's 1988–89 second-grade class at Dresden Elementary School in Dresden, Tennessee, "adopted" an elderly neighbor and provided services such as grocery shopping, lawn care, and friendly visits. This class won a Kids Care Contest merit award for its project.

Citizenship Goals
To recognize that different people have different needs; to realize that friends can be any age.

Preparation
Identify an elderly neighbor or couple who would like assistance in everyday and special tasks.

Procedure
1. As a class, meet with your neighbor. Talk about ways that you can help, for example, by grocery shopping, getting mail, raking leaves, planting flowers, picking up and returning library books, and visiting.
2. Set up a schedule of activities. What will you do, how often, and when? Don't forget holidays and birthdays.

Modification
Reinforce not only that friends can be different ages but can have different abilities, too. Do this by adapting your project to help out a neighbor who has a handicapping condition that makes everyday activities difficult, or who recently underwent an operation and is still recuperating.

Extension Activities
Science/Math/Art: Plan a special spring treat for your neighbor—a flower garden. Research plants that grow well in your area. Plan an activity such as a can recycling drive to raise money to purchase gardening materials. How many cans will you need to collect and recycle? As landscape architects, have students diagram where the flowers will go before planting and caring for them.

Social Development: Help your students and their neighbor get to know one another better by inviting your new friend in to share a hobby, a favorite story, or a lesson about his or her area of expertise.

Read-Along Books for Pediatric Patients

Project Goal
To make pediatric patients' hospital stays more tolerable.

Project Summary
Dorian Colvin's 1989–90 first-grade students at Kashmere Gardens Elementary School in Houston, Texas, wrote, illustrated, and taped read-along books for pediatric patients at an area hospital. The books' shapes reflected their topics; for example, one was shaped like a hot-air balloon, one like a dog, and one like a train.

Citizenship Goals
To work cooperatively toward a common goal, and to become more sensitive to the needs of others.

Preparation
Brainstorm a list of topics for your read-along books. Decide how many read-along books you can produce and take a class vote to select topics. Gather materials for your project, including book-quality paper, crayons, markers, blank cassette tapes, and tape recorders.

Procedure
1. Have students cooperatively write and illustrate a story based on one of the selected topics. (You might have each student write and illustrate one page of the book or divide students into groups to accomplish different parts of the process.)
2. After editing the story line and finalizing illustrations, students should produce a final version of the book, designed to reflect the topic. (For example, if students are writing a story about ocean life, they might cut book pages in the shape of a whale.)
3. Have students tape the text of the book. Package the book and tape to make a read-along book.
4. Repeat steps 1 through 3 with new topics to produce additional read-along books.
5. Donate the books to pediatric patients at a local hospital.

Extension Activity
Language Arts: Read a book about hospitals, such as *Things to Know before You Go to the Hospital* by Lisa Ann Marsoli (Silver Burdett, 1985). Have students write their own books about going to the hospital, using student interviews to gather information.

TeleCare

Project Goal
To provide a service for elderly people living alone.

Project Summary
Dian Wurst's 1988–89 third-grade students at Polk-Hordville Public School in Polk, Nebraska, started a telephone service called TeleCare. They teamed up with elderly people living alone and called every morning just to see if everything was okay. If there was a problem they called for help. They won a Kids Care Contest grand prize for their project.

Citizenship Goal
To recognize that they are capable of helping people with special needs.

Preparation
Check with a local senior center, students' parents, churches, and synagogues to identify elderly people in your community who live alone and would like to participate in TeleCare. Obtain necessary information for each participant: telephone number, address, and name and telephone number of a friend or relative who can be contacted if help is needed.

Create a weekly or monthly record sheet with above information. Include space to record daily comments, for example, Mrs. Turner answered the phone and everything's fine.

Pair each student with a TeleCare partner. Assign backups for each day of the week to make calls for students who are absent on any given day. Obtain the use of at least one telephone each morning for a specified period of time—try to get a wireless telephone so that children can remain in the classroom while placing calls. Set up a schedule for making phone calls. Make sure the people you will be contacting are aware of the time at which they can expect calls.

Procedure
1. Every weekday morning at a specified time, students take turns making telephone calls to each participant. Students greet their telephone pals, identify themselves, and ask if everything is okay. If something is wrong, students call the friend or relative listed for help, or follow other procedures as indicated.
2. As each call is completed, the student placing the call initials the log and records remarks about the call. ("Everything's fine." or "Mr. Putnam didn't answer after two tries so I called his sister.")
3. Double check records daily to make sure everyone gets a call.

Modification
If your class is unable to set up a system of daily telephone calls to elderly people in your community, you can help in other ways. For example, set

up a system of letter-writing and have groups of students take turns writing each week. Or if your elderly partners have tape recorders, communicate orally through audiotapes. Have students invite their partners to "talk back!"

Extension Activities

Civic: Team up with a high school class to help them get a TeleCare service going for more members of your community.

Social Studies/Math: Obtain results of the 1990 census. Have students determine how many elderly people live in the United States. How many live alone? Have students compare this information with results from the previous census. How have the numbers changed? Have students graph both sets of information. Discuss possible reasons for the most significant differences between the two sets of information.

Language Arts: Get an autobiography exchange going. Have your students begin by writing something about themselves. For example, they might write about the most important event in their lives to date. Have students send these beginnings to their TeleCare pals who can write on the same topic on the same piece of paper. Have students continue exchanging stories with their new friends, each week writing another segment of their autobiographies.

2

Community Involvement

Projects to build a better community—from promoting traffic safety to restoring an historical landmark.

> Adopt a Window
>
> Bear Necessities
>
> Bricks for Books
>
> Fire Safety
>
> Footsteps Into Our Past
>
> Knowing the Facts
>
> Making History
>
> New Life for Books
>
> Sharing School with Sick Kids
>
> Stop, Look, Walk
>
> Welcome to Our Community

Adopt a Window

Project Goal
To beautify your community by cleaning up and creating monthly displays for a window in an abandoned or unrented building.

Project Summary
JoAnn Christoffersen's 1990–91 third-grade students and Linda Peterson's 1990–91 fifth-grade students at Lyons-Decatur Northeast Schools in Lyons, Nebraska, adopted a window in an abandoned building. They created different window displays each month.

Citizenship Goal
To take pride in your surroundings.

Preparation
Have students look for abandoned buildings with windows low and large enough to be cleaned up and decorated. Check with local realtors and town officials to get permission for your project and access to the building you choose.

Procedure
1. Make arrangements to clean up the area directly behind the windows.
2. Brainstorm window display themes. Consider displays with educational purposes, for example to promote AIDS awareness, literacy, or good health and fitness habits.
3. Set up a schedule of displays. Assign teams of students to create each display or have the class work together on each.

Modification
Get permission to adopt the side of an abandoned building to beautify with an educational mural. Plan a design that will express the message of your choice. For example, if you want to encourage children to make healthy choices in their lives regarding drugs, you could combine a slogan with scenes that show children involved in positive activities.

Extension Activities
Social Studies/Language Arts: Use your local newspaper's real-estate section to learn more about the real-estate situation in your town. Have each student choose a piece of property he or she feels will be the most difficult to rent or sell and write an advertisement to attract takers.

Science/Art: Birds are often injured by flying unwittingly into windows. Prevent this from happening at your school by making cut-paper designs to place in windows.

Bear Necessities

Project Goal
To give comfort to kids in emergency situations.

Project Summary
Beverley Gilmore and Lois Collier's 1989–90 fifth-grade students at Eagle Hill Middle School in Manlius, New York, raised money to buy teddy bears for their police department. The bears are carried in local police cars to comfort children in crisis situations.

Citizenship Goal
To empathize with problems of one's peers.

Preparation
Contact your local police department to discuss your class project. Prepare a lesson on the history of teddy bears, dating back to Teddy Roosevelt. Show examples of different bears produced over the years. Familiarize yourself and your students with the organization "The Good Bears of the World" (see Resources). Organize fund-raising projects to raise money for the purchase of bears.

Procedure
1. Make posters that explain and advertise your fund-raising project.
2. Hold your fund-raising event. Include a display about the bear project so that patrons can learn more.
3. Present your proceeds to "The Good Bears of the World" in exchange for teddy bears.
4. Arrange to present the bears to the police department.

Extension Activities

Language Arts: Have each student bring teddy bears to class, exchange his or her bear with another student, bring that bear home for one week, and keep a daily journal of adventures that teddy bear had while at a new home.

Math: The Alaskan brown bear may weigh up to 1,700 pounds. Approximately how many students in your class will it take to equal the weight of the bear?

Dramatic Arts: Have students give dramatic readings of the story *The Three Bears*. Have them experiment with pitch and expression as they play the parts of each bear.

Bricks for Books

Project Goal
To help build an addition to the community library so that people can more easily access books and materials.

Project Summary
Mary Nicolais, Linda Schuller, and Patricia Williams's 1990–91 first-grade students at South Abington School in Chinchilla, Pennsylvania, organized a "Buy a Brick" campaign to raise more than $1,500 for an addition to the community library. They sold construction paper bricks for $1 each, wrote the donors' names on them, and displayed them in classroom windows so that everyone could watch the building progress. They won a Kids Care Contest merit award for their project.

Citizenship Goal
To care about what is happening in your community.

Preparation
Take a class trip to the library. Discuss different purposes of a library. How is it an important part of your community?

Procedure
1. Cut out as many bricks as you need to sell to meet your goal.
2. Arrange visits to each class and office during which time your students outline the project and answer questions.
3. Design and send home fliers explaining the project.
4. Make posters presenting project details. Display them in banks, post offices, and grocery stores.
5. As donors buy bricks, write their names on the bricks and tape the bricks to classroom windows.
6. Report daily totals during morning announcements. Keep a pictograph of your progress in the lobby or library.

Modification
If your community library doesn't need additional space at this time, expand it in other ways. For example, donate an environmental education section—purchasing resources that offer information on a variety of issues, tips, and activities for taking environmental action. Make a special effort to include materials for kids.

Extension Activity
Science/Math: Take a community survey. What are most of the buildings in your community constructed from? Graph results and discuss reasons for a predominance of any one building material.

Fire Safety

Project Goals
To learn about fire safety; to obtain fire equipment for the community.

Project Summary
Dave Maze's 1989–90 third- and fourth-grade students at Z. J. Williams School in Napaskiak, Alaska, opened a school store to raise money to buy fire equipment for their community. They also requested used equipment from fire departments across the country, and applied for and won a national grant. They won a Kids Care Contest grand prize for their project.

Citizenship Goal
To recognize kids' participation in community improvement.

Preparation
Examine your community's fire-safety program. Discuss whether or not the community's fire-safety program is adequate. Make a list of your fire department's needs (specific equipment, more fire fighters, and so on). Research the cost. Decide on a plan of action.

Procedure
1. Write to the governor and other state officials expressing concern over the community's fire-safety program or facilities and requesting funds to make the necessary purchases. Include estimated costs.
2. Write to fire departments across the country asking for donations of used equipment; apply for grants from community and regional affairs offices; set up fund-raising projects to raise additional funds.

Modification
Ask your local police chief for a list of badge numbers and names of all the police officers in your community. Have each student adopt an officer and write letters to him or her. This will help students develop a sense of respect for the officers and will make them aware of the many jobs in the police department. Arrange for officers to visit your class or for a class trip to the police station.

Extension Activity
Math: Have each student map out a fire-escape route from the classroom to a safe spot outdoors. Using a stop watch, time how long it takes students to follow their safety routes. Compare student plans with the school plan.

Modification idea from Sr. Ellen McKeon, A.S.C.J., and her 1989–90 fifth-grade students at St. Rocco's School, Johnston, Rhode Island.

Footsteps Into Our Past

Project Goal
To honor local immigrants and recognize personal heritage.

Project Summary
Sharon Appleby's 1990–91 fourth-grade students at C. E. Cole Intermediate School in Laureldale, Pennsylvania, created a museum, Footsteps Into Our Past, to display information about their ancestors and to honor local immigrants. The museum opened for the three days preceding Thanksgiving and the public was invited to visit and to record names and homelands of local immigrants. The information was inscribed on a plaque and displayed in the community library.

Citizenship Goals
To recognize the importance of immigration in our history and to understand what the Bill of Rights means to all U.S. citizens.

Preparation
Discuss terms that are an integral part of this project—*immigration, emigration, naturalization, heritage, ancestry, archives,* and *artifacts*. Talk about some of the countries students' ancestors emigrated from. Locate these countries on a map. Trace routes from these countries to Ellis Island. Now trace the route from Ellis Island to your town.

Procedure
1. As a class activity, make a list of questions students have about their ancestors' homelands. For example, they might want to know what schools were like, what kinds of toys kids played with, what a typical home was like, and what kind of governments countries had. Have them include more specific questions—What did my great-grandparents do? How did they earn a living? What were they hoping for in America? Talk about what makes a good interview question—those that can be answered with a yes or no might not yield the desired information.
2. Have students use these questions to interview parents, grandparents, and other relatives. Suggest several methods for recording the interviews—taking notes, audiotaping, or videotaping.
3. Have students write stories about their ancestors and their homelands, including quotes when possible.
4. Write a letter to parents explaining the project and requesting items that support students' understanding of their heritage for display in the museum. Immigration papers, clothing, dolls, letters, coins, packaged foods, musical instruments, photographs, and postcards are some possibilities.
5. Talk about what the United States Bill of Rights means to immigrants. Discuss, for example, how freedom of speech might be a new freedom for some immigrants. Make a poster-size copy of the Bill of Rights for display at the museum.

6. Put together a series of special performances for your exhibit. Share videotaped interviews; create dramatizations of life in some of the countries featured at the museum or about Ellis Island; perform traditional songs or model traditional dress.

7. Create posters inviting your community to the museum. Display them in prominent places around town. Send invitations to other classes, school and district personnel, students' families, local newspapers and television stations, and town officials. Include museum dates and hours, location, and a schedule of special performances.

8. Make these final preparations for opening day:
- Prepare a book for visitors to record the names of local immigrants they know. (After the exhibit you can have the names inscribed on a plaque or record them yourselves on a scroll. Donate or lend that and the book to a library or historical society.)
- Create and display signs welcoming visitors and directing them to different sections of the museum.
- Solicit help from community volunteers to prepare samples of traditional food to share with visitors at an opening reception.
- Assign museum jobs to students such as curator, reception hosts, information assistants, guides, and guards.
- Finally, display the works and get ready to welcome your visitors!

Modification

You'll probably find that some students have realtives living elsewhere in the country. They can conduct interviews by corresponding with letters or by exchanging audiotapes.

Extension Activities

Language Arts: Rewrite the Bill of Rights in language that we might use today; for example, instead of "The enumeration in the Constitution of certain rights shall not be construed to deny or disparage others retained by the people," the ninth amendment might read, "People's rights are not limited to the ones listed in the Bill of Rights."

Social Studies: Create a computer database of students in your school who are from other countries. First invite them to your class one at a time to discuss their homelands. Enter their names, grades, nationalities, and special interests into a database. As your class studies other countries, have students use the database as a resource to locate schoolmates who can help them better understand the people, customs, culture, and geography of a particular country.

Art: Have students create flags representing their heritage. Display finished flags, then have students combine elements from each to create a class flag representing all students' ancestries.

Knowing the Facts

Project Goal
To share information about AIDS with other students.

Project Summary
D.D. Brown's 1990-91 sixth-grade students at P.S. 144, M, in New York City, made posters to inform students about AIDS. They also wrote a book, *Do You Know the Facts...* which was presented to each class, along with an oral presentation on AIDS.

Citizenship Goal
To learn that sharing knowledge with other children is rewarding as well as being a learning vehicle.

Preparation
Pass out an index card to each student. Tell them not to put their names on them, but to write down any questions they may have about AIDS. Prepare several lessons on AIDS, answering as many student questions as possible. Invite a health care professional to your classroom to provide additional information.

Procedure
1. Decide which student questions are likely to be shared by other students. Make and display posters that ask and answer these questions.
2. Before beginning the book on facts about AIDS, separate the class into several groups. Have students volunteer to work on various parts of the book, including: What is AIDS?, The History of AIDS, Who Gets AIDS?, Precautions, Wrong Ideas about AIDS, Is There a Cure for AIDS?, a glossary, and any other sections they feel should be included. Have students include illustrations to go with the facts.
3. Have students present their book along with an oral presentation to other classes. Display a copy in the library.

Extension Activities
Language Arts: Have students do research, then give a presentation or write a book, play, or poem on a disease or social concern to help inform other students of important health issues.

Math: Find out the number of AIDS cases that have been reported over the past decade. Graph your statistics. What conclusions can be made from looking at your graph? In what year were the most cases reported?

Careers: Invite health care professionals to your classroom to speak about different career choices in the medical and health care fields.

Modification idea from Lee Freeman, C. Garner, and E. Tooson's 1988–89 third-grade students at Stafford Elementary School in Tuscaloosa, Alabama.

Making History

Project Goals
To develop a consideration and appreciation for the buildings and landmarks in a community; to call attention to people at a grass-roots level who are making contributions to the community.

Project Summary
Debbie Lerner and Punky Beasley's 1988–89 kindergarten through fifth-grade students at Red Bridge Elementary School and P.S.I. Elementary in Kansas City, Missouri, studied the architectural, historical, environmental, social, and economic facets of their city. The students visited landmarks in their city. Then they put together a calendar of Kansas City landmarks. To help kick off a campaign to save one of their city's historic landmarks, the students sang a song about the landmark.

Citizen Goal
To develop a sense of pride in one's city.

Preparation
Have students study the backgrounds, architecture, function, and so on of community landmarks. Try to obtain historic photos or models of the buildings.

Procedure
1. Take several walking tours of the city to view landmarks. Discuss each landmark's architectural elements—building materials, roof, windows, doors, decorative motifs, function, its environment, and changes that have occurred in the area and to the building. Bring paper and drawing pencils on your visits to record impressions.
2. Have students create sketches of each landmark. Select one sketch of each landmark to be refined for the calendar.
3. Working from sketches, existing models, and photos, have students whose work was chosen for the calendar redraw their buildings to fit on 8 ½-by-11-inch paper. Make sure they sign their artwork. Have other students turn sketches into a collage for front and back covers.
4. Have one group of students label the architectural elements of each building drawing while a second group types up definitions of each element for a calendar Glossary of Architectural Terms.
5. Have students write the name of the building, the architect's name, and the building address on each of the twelve drawings.
6. Choose which building will be featured each month. On the pages opposite the drawings, lay out a monthly calendar. Create decorative borders.
7. Once a sample calendar is completed, have students take advance orders. Photocopy the number of copies you need onto sturdy card stock. Bind pages together using a binding machine or metal fasteners. Drill a hole in each calendar for hanging.

8. Distribute advance order copies. Mail copies of the calendars with cover letters to the owners and managers of each building, the mayor, the historical society, and the library. Sell additional copies to community members. Donate the proceeds to help restore a landmark that needs repair.

Modification

Select a statue in your community that you like. Learn about its history, significance, and reasons it was erected. If you could choose an event or person to dedicate a statue to, who would you choose? Where would the statue be placed?

Extension Activities:

Social Studies: Design awards to give to community members who have made a contribution to your community, such as planting a garden, designing an interesting building, improving a shopping center site.

Art: Using cardboard boxes and other scrap materials, create a replica of the downtown area of your city. Include "cardboard" models of your city's landmarks.

Geography: Have students study a map of your city. Ask them to draw a walking-tour map that shows the locations of your city's landmarks.

Math: Using marshmallows, gumdrops, toothpicks, and raw spaghetti strands, have kids build tall, sturdy towers. Emphasize the importance of using measurement and basic geometry skills, and incorporating their new knowledge of architecture.

New Life for Books

Project Goal
To encourage children's love of literature and care of library books.

Project Summary
Cynthia Eschenmann's 1989–90 fourth-grade students at Annville Elementary in Annville, Pennsylvania, wrote reviews of selected books for the children's library. Students made covers for books with unattractive or damaged covers, and took responsibility for caring for the shelves.

Citizenship Goal
To view "volunteerism" as opposed to "earning money," as a worthwhile contribution to a community.

Preparation
Obtain permission for your project from your school librarian or public library. Ask the librarian to speak to students about caring for shelves and books. Have him or her assign each student a shelf to care for.

Procedure
1. As students write literary reviews of books that they've read, post them in the library to encourage other kids to read.
2. Working with the librarian, have students select books that could use new covers. Have students design new covers for these books.
3. Once a month, have students care for, clean, and alphabetize their shelves.

Modification
To help interest young readers in books, each month have students paint characters from their favorite books to hang in the children's section of your public library.

Extension Activities
Art: Ask each student to choose a favorite library book and design a book display using an empty cereal box. Here's how: Measure out enough paper to cover the entire box. Before covering the box, use crayons or colored pencils to illustrate a favorite scene from the story. Add the title, author, and illustrator. Attach the paper to the cereal box and display in the library to help promote reading.

Dramatic Arts: Have students dress up as their favorite book characters. Videotape them giving book reviews, book talks, or storytellings.

Modification idea from Darlene Considine's 1988–89 first-grade students at Spring Grove Elementary School, Spring Grove, Illinois.

Sharing School With Sick Kids

Project Goal
To brighten the lives of seriously ill children in the hospital.

Project Summary
Uvonne Morris's 1988–89 second-grade students at Joseph J. Rhoads Elementary School in Houston, Texas, made monthly videotapes of classroom activities to share with children hospitalized with serious illnesses. They won a Kids Care Contest merit award for their project.

Citizenship Goal
To recognize sharing as a way to help others.

Preparation
Team up with a local hospital. If the hospital does not have a VCR, solicit a donor or lender. Obtain a camera to film class activities.

Procedure
1. Discuss the parts of your day that other children might be interested in sharing. Identify upcoming events that you know you'll want to videotape, such as a dramatic arts performance or a field trip. Make a filming schedule for each month.
2. Prepare and tape an initial activity to introduce class members to kids in the hospital. Follow up with activities as planned.
3. Deliver the videotape each month. Include letters to the kids, too.

Modification
If videotape equipment is unavailable, create and send activity books to kids in the hospital. Discuss the kinds of activities you want to include, such as joke pages, word searches, mazes, word games, story starters, and picture starters. Have each student create a page. Photocopy and collate pages to make books, and send them off to the children's unit.

Extension Activities
Social Studies: Compare the most common illnesses and diseases of children in other countries with U.S. statistics. What could explain the similarities? The differences?

Art/Language Arts: Have each student design a hospital just for kids, creating a detailed drawing of the plan and writing a description of why this should be the way hospital communities are built for kids.

Stop, Look, Walk

Project Goals
To increase awareness of crosswalk and traffic safety; to develop good safety habits.

Project Summary
Timothy Sullivan's 1988–89 sixth-grade students at Conant Elementary in Concord, New Hampshire, spray-painted the words "Stop, Look, Walk" on every street corner in their school district. This project was adopted after a classmate was killed while crossing the street on his way home from school. They won a Kids Care Contest grand prize for their project.

Citizenship Goals
To develop a sense of community and to promote traffic safety.

Preparation
Before beginning this project, get permission from the city (try contacting your city director or mayor's office). Decide on the letter size, color, and locations of the words you will paint. Purchase spray paint and posterboard for stencils. Solicit parent volunteers to supervise painting expeditions. Practice using spray paint. Set up a time each week for parents and students to paint their designated corners.

Procedure
1. To make a stencil, write the words "Stop, Look, Walk" (or other safety message) on a piece of sturdy posterboard. Cut out each letter.
2. Divide your class into groups. Give each a stencil, spray paint, a map indicating their designated corners, and a parent volunteer.
3. Have students and volunteers spray paint their designated corners.

Modification
Organize a bike-skills rodeo (see Resources) that focuses on bicycle safety. Set up a series of stations. At each station, kids will perform certain bicycle skills such as hand signals, looking back without swerving, or weaving around traffic cones.

Extension Activities
Social Studies: Show pictures of street signs and have students identify each one and explain what it means. You may want to show each sign in black and white and have students guess what color each sign is.

Language Arts: Read a book about safety such as *Safety Can Be Fun* by Munro Leaf (Trophy Harper, 1988). Discuss ways students can keep safe.

Geography: Draw a map of the streets around your school. Fill in all the safety signs you can find. Talk about the purpose of each sign.

Welcome to Our Community

Project Goals
To help new residents of a community learn about family-oriented resources, activities, and establishments available and to promote an atmosphere of acceptance and community among all residents.

Project Summary
Carol Ward's 1988–89 third-grade students at Carthage Elementary School in Carthage, New York, wanted to help the many new families moving into their area as the Fort Drum military installation expanded. To welcome these families to their community and to help them feel more quickly at home, they created a Kids Care Welcome Book.

Citizenship Goal
To recognize community needs and to work together to provide solutions.

Preparation
Have students prepare a list of community facilities (such as libraries, zoos, parks, and playgrounds), activities (such as recreation programs, youth groups, and the 4-H Club), points of interest (such as historical sites, district schools, and museums) and establishments (such as family-style restaurants, video rental stores, and bookstores that are especially appealing and/or helpful to kids and their families. Include information on the district's schools, too.

Write a class letter to each explaining your project. Request information to share with families that are new to the area. Write the chamber of commerce and request a map of the community to reproduce in your book.

Procedure
1. Discuss responses to your written requests for information. Develop a master list of the facilities, activities, attractions, and establishments you'll include in the book.
2. Have students work in teams to write and illustrate each section of the book. Include a book cover design, an introduction, and an index of places mentioned as group assignments.
3. Obtain permission to reproduce a map of your town (or draw one) and mark each place mentioned in the book.
4. Reproduce, collate, and staple book pages.
5. Make copies of the book available to your district office for distribution to new residents enrolling children in your school, to military housing developments (if applicable), to the chamber of commerce, to information centers, and to your local library.
6. Send copies to all who responded to your initial request for information.

Modification

Promote school unity by sponsoring a welcome breakfast once a month or once a semester for all new students in your school. Invite new students, students who attended the last welcome breakfast as new students, students from different grades who have been in the area a while, and various staff members.

Extension Activities

Math/Language Arts: Take a school survey. Ask: How many times have you moved in your lifetime? In the past five years? Average and graph the results by individual grades and for the entire school. Talk about some of the reasons families move. Follow this up with a class survey: If you could live in any state, which one would you choose? Write a class "press release" announcing kids' top ten choices.

Social Studies: Consider the case of the Fort Drum expansion. Over a period of five years, 30,000 new people would move into the area, including 8,000 children. If 30,000 people moved into your town over a period of five years, how would schooling, housing, employment, business, and the overall economy be affected? For example, what kinds of businesses might open in response to the expansion? What kinds of problems might be created by increased population? If you were a superintendent, how would you accommodate so many new students? If you were a teacher, what would you worry about?

3

Social Action

Projects to help solve the problems of hunger, homelessness, poverty, illiteracy, and drug abuse—from growing potatoes for people who don't have enough to eat to helping families build homes.

Crop Walk

Harvest for Hunger

Help Build a House

Keep Them Warm

Mayflower Card Company

Operation Brown Paper Bag

Quilt for the Community

Shops for Shelters

Stamp Out Drugs

Stone Soup

Crop Walk

Project Goal
To develop an awareness of and to fight world hunger.

Project Summary
Carolyn Rodgers's 1987–88 third-grade students at Monroe Elementary in Norman, Oklahoma, participated in an event called Crop Walk. For every mile they walked, sponsors donated money. The class earned more than $600 to help feed people who do not have enough to eat and helped prepare, serve, and clean up at a free lunch in their town.

Citizenship Goal
To recognize that sometimes people need to be made aware of problems and that, if asked, they are often willing to help.

Preparation
Find out about participating in a walk-a-thon such as Crop Walk. If there's not one in your area, organize one.

Procedure
1. Have students ask friends and family members to sponsor them in the walk-a-thon by pledging a certain amount of money for each mile walked. (Use sign-up sheets.)
2. After the walk, collect pledges. Donate them to the sponsoring organization. If you planned your own, donate proceeds to an organization that works to alleviate hunger.
3. Volunteer to prepare, serve, and clean up at a local soup kitchen.

Modification
Prepare a meal for the hungry in your community. Plan a menu. Figure out how much of each ingredient you will need. Have each student bring in a certain quantity of food. Serve your meal at a homeless shelter, school lunchroom, or community center.

Extension Activities
Math: Check an almanac to find the population of several countries. Find out how many people in each country are affected by hunger. Graph the total population and total number of people affected by hunger in each country.

Language Arts: Put together a book of each student's family's favorite recipe. Sell copies to friends, relatives, and other community members. Donate the proceeds to help feed hungry people.

Modification idea from Sandra Epstein's 1990–91 fifth-grade students, Hawthorn Intermediate, Vernon Hills, Illinois.

Harvest for Hunger

Project Goal
To make a significant contribution to feeding people who do not have enough to eat.

Project Summary
Robbie McHardy's 1988–89 first-grade students at Louisiana State University Laboratory School in Baton Rouge, Louisiana, planted, tended, and harvested a 300-foot garden, and donated 365 pounds of potatoes to a local food bank. They won a Kids Care Contest grand prize for this project.

Citizenship Goals
To increase awareness about other's needs and to recognize that people contribute in different ways to solve problems.

Preparation
Begin preparing for this project well in advance, in order to be prepared for planting when the time comes. First, locate a large plot of land for your gardening project. You might request permission to start a permanent garden on school grounds, get a neighbor with lots of land to donate a portion for your project, or check with town officials about converting an abandoned lot into a garden. Next, round up gardening materials. Have a plant sale to raise money for other supplies.

Procedure
1. Invite a horticulturalist to talk with your students about gardening. Discuss preparing soil, germinating seeds, transplanting seedlings, fertilizing, watering, weeding, and composting.
2. With the horticulturalist's help, choose the crop or crops you'll raise. Consider what grows best in your area, what will produce the most amount of food for the space, and what can best be used by the food pantry.
3. When it's planting time in your area, divide the class into teams, each responsible for planting, maintaining, and harvesting a section of the garden.
4. After harvesting your crop, sort the fruit or vegetables and deliver them to the food bank. (Make sure to arrange for delivery first so they can make room, if need be, for your donation.)

Modification
You can harvest food in your own cafeteria, too. Students might be surprised at the amount of unopened, prepackaged food, and whole, fresh fruit that is thrown away each day in their cafeteria. Organize a drive to collect this food. Label and decorate boxes for this food and place them next to the cafeteria trash cans. Station student volunteers next to them the first few days to help other kids learn what goes

where. Make arrangements to deliver the food on a regular basis to a local food pantry or homeless shelter.

Extension Activities

Science: Experiment with different ways to grow potatoes—from seed or from potato pieces. Plant potato pieces (with at least one eye) in one pot. Plant potato seeds in another. When sprouts appear, thin the seedlings to one per pot. Observe growth in each pot. Which method do you think farmers prefer? Why?

Social Studies: Research the history of potatoes and develop a list of fun facts about this food crop, for example "they" are about 80 percent water and 20 percent solid matter. Design a bulletin-board display to share these facts without naming the food. Challenge students in your school to name the food crop.

Math: Examine a bagful of potatoes. Compute the average number of potatoes you could grow using the potatoes in this bag. (Hint: Kids will have to count the eyes on each potato.)

Science: Ask students to imagine that, from this year on, only three kinds of fruits and/or vegetables can be grown. Divide students into teams and have them decide which three crops they would choose. Allow time for research, and encourage students to give sound reasoning for their choices.

Modification idea from Ruth Struglinski's 1987–88 fourth-grade students, Bath Elementary School, Akron, Ohio, Kids Care Contest merit winner.

Help Build a House

Project Goal
To provide building supplies to help build a house for a family.

Project Summary
Kathy Ciolino and Gretchen Stuempfle's 1990–91 first-grade students at Keefauver Elementary School in Gettysburg, Pennsylvania, collected building materials for Habitat for Humanity, a nonprofit organization that builds housing for families in need. They won a Kids Care Contest merit award for this project.

Citizenship Goal
To learn that when many people contribute small amounts, great goals can be realized.

Preparation
Read *The President Builds a House* by Tom Shelton (Simon & Schuster, 1989) to learn about the work of Habitat for Humanity and Jimmy Carter's involvement in the organization.

Procedure
1. Brainstorm a list of building materials that students can gather to help Habitat for Humanity families build their homes, for example, disposable nose masks, pencils, nails (8P or 16P), fine sandpaper (#200), wood glue, masking tape, flat head screws.
2. Together, write a letter to students' families telling them about Habitat for Humanity and your class project. List items you hope to collect and request that each child be allowed to contribute a small donation. Include a deadline for donations.
3. Invite a member of Habitat for Humanity to visit your class to talk about the organization's work, answer questions, and accept students' donations.

Modification
You can also buy a particular item for a Habitat for Humanity house. For example, research the cost of a front door, a window, or a kitchen sink. Organize a recycling drive to raise the money.

Extension Activities
Social Studies: Send students on a search in their classroom for supplies used to build their classroom. Compare lists and count up the total number of materials used to build your classroom.

Language Arts: Explore the concept of homes with *A House Is a House for Me* by Mary Ann Hoberman (Penguin USA, 1978). As a pre-reading activity, challenge students to think of objects or places that serve as houses.

Keep Them Warm

Project Goal
To increase students' awareness of the needs of homeless people.

Project Summary
Barb Tigges and Mary Beth Reiff's 1990–91 third-grade students at Sacred Heart School in Des Moines, Iowa, held a coat and blanket drive. All of the coats and blankets they collected were distributed to the homeless and underprivileged people in their community. They won a Kids Care Contest grand prize for their project.

Citizenship Objective
Students will learn that they can make a difference in the lives of others.

Preparation
Discuss being homeless. Ask local dry cleaners to volunteer to clean the coats that students collect. Set up a schedule for dropping off and picking up the coats. Arrange to distribute the coats and blankets through a local homeless organization.

Procedure
1. Have students create fliers and posters, and write newspaper articles to spread the word about their coat and blanket drive.
2. Keep a tally of the number of coats and blankets collected. At the end of each week, bring the coats to the participating dry cleaners, and then distribute them as planned.
3. Invite an official to the classroom to speak about homelessness.
4. Visit a homeless shelter. Volunteer to help serve a meal or bake cookies.

Extension Activities
Math: Have students bake cookies to bring to a homeless shelter. Find out how many people need to be served (or how many you can afford to serve). Ask students to determine whether the cookie recipe needs to be doubled, tripled, or quadrupled. Have them recalculate the proportions of ingredients accordingly.

Social Studies: The Bill of Rights stipulates certain inalienable rights for all Americans. Do students think the right to a home should be included in the Constitution? Have students pretend they are lawmakers drafting a Constitutional amendment that guarantees a home for all people. Take a class vote on the amendment.

Art: Laminate both sides of rectangular or oval placemat-sized drawings. Deliver the placemats to a local soup kitchen.

Mayflower Card Company

Project Goals
To learn the importance of economics in the lives of American citizens; to make holidays more meaningful by focusing on the needs of others.

Project Summary
Barbara Harlan's 1990–91 third-grade students at East Side Elementary in Jacksonville, Texas, formed the Mayflower Card Company. They created original Thanksgiving cards and bookmarks which were sold to family, students, and school staff. The proceeds were used to help needy children.

Citizenship Goals
To know that good citizenship includes learning about the American economic system; to understand that a successful business involves planning, teamwork, and a cooperative spirit; expressing love and appreciation and to realize that meeting the needs of others is what holidays are all about.

Preparation
Explain your project to a local bank. Arrange for each student to get a $1 loan in exchange for some form of "collateral" (for example a doll or trading cards). Decide what materials you will need to purchase in order to set up your holiday card business. Vote on a company name.

Procedure
1. On the designated day, students bring their "collateral" to school. Then take a trip to the participating bank for the loans.
2. Purchase supplies with the borrowed money.
3. Set aside time each day for students to make the cards. Have them sketch their ideas on scrap paper before actually making the cards.
4. Make posters and fliers to advertise the card sale. Offer to make special orders.
5. Plan to start selling the cards about two weeks before Thanksgiving. Set up a table at certain times during school hours when the cards can be sold to students.
6. Keep a record of how mnay are sold.
7. When the sale is over, visit the bank to pay back the loan and collect the students' "collateral."
8. Donate the profits to an organization that helps needy people.

Modification
Students can use construction paper to draw and cut out Thanksgiving symbols, such as pilgrims and turkeys. Glue each one on an ice-cream stick to make Thanksgiving puppets. Have students write an original Thanksgiving skit. For admission to the performance, have other

students and parents bring canned goods. Take the food to a local shelter, food pantry, or someplace where it will be distributed to needy families. These projects can be adapted to any holiday.

Extension Activities

Language Arts: Have students recycle old greeting cards to make new cards. Students can cut the backs off of greeting cards and paste the artwork to the front of folded construction paper. Students can write original verses inside the cards.

Math: Help students develop fiscal plans for their card company. Have children calculate how many cards they will need to sell at what price to pay off their loans. Then have students set a reasonable goal of how much money they'd like to raise above costs. Help them determine how many more cards they'll have to sell to reach their goal.

Social Studies: Talk about the role of food in Thanksgiving celebrations. Have students bring in recipes for some of the foods their families serve at Thanksgiving dinner. Students can then compile their recipes to make books. Have students design colorful covers for the recipe books, then sell them along with their holiday cards to help raise money.

Art: Have students cut cornucopia shapes out of colored construction paper and paste each on another piece of paper. Then have students cut out words and pictures from magazines and newspapers of all the things for which they are thankful. Have students paste the pictures and words inside their cornucopias.

Operation Brown Paper Bag

Project Goal
To supply a food pantry with paper bags for distributing food to people who do not have enough to eat.

Project Summary
Ann Dauer's 1990–91 fifth-grade students at Valley View Elementary School in Green Bay, Wisconsin, organized a schoolwide brown paper bag drive. They collected and sorted 2,800 bags and gave them to a food pantry. The food pantry used the bags to distribute food to people who don't have enough to eat. They won a Kids Care Contest merit award.

Citizenship Goal
To realize that people can help others without any cost involved.

Preparation
Team up with a food bank, pantry, or other organization that uses bags to distribute food or clothing. Find out how many and what kind they need, and when they are most needed.

Procedure
1. Find a safe place to store bags as they are collected.
2. Decide on a collection procedure. Pick up bags from classrooms once a week or designate a central drop-off location.
3. Design a campaign to inform students, staff, and the community of the project. For example, write and perform a rap over the P.A., design posters, and publish a newsletter to distribute in the community.
4. As students collect bags, have them count and sort them.
5. Deliver bags, as arranged, to the food pantry.

Modification
Join forces with a grocery store to support food banks in a different way. Ask the store to donate a can of food to a food bank for every bag students decorate.

Extension Activities
Math: Make a giant paper bag pictograph and display it in the lobby, library, cafeteria, or main office. Have students graph progress by tens, hundreds, or some other number of bags collected.

Science: If it takes one 15- to 20-year-old tree to make 700 paper bags, how many trees did Ann Dauer's class save? How many can your school save?

Modification idea from Debora Mackiel's 1988–89 fourth/fifth-grade students at Oak Valley Elementary School in Omaha, Nebraska—Kids Care Contest merit winners.

Quilt for the Community

Project Goal
To help a community food pantry serve people in need.

Project Summary
Margaret Kuhfeld's 1990–91 sixth-grade students at Brimhall Elementary School in Roseville, Minnesota, designed and made a quilt reflecting their state. They raffled off the quilt and donated the proceeds to a local food pantry.

Citizenship Goal
To recognize that there are many different ways people can contribute to solving a single problem.

Preparation
Have students decide how big they want each quilt square and calculate how much material they'll need for the entire quilt, front and back. Gather quilting materials, including cloth, thread, batting, fabric paint or markers, and string. Check with a fabric store for more details. Finance the materials by either paying for them and reimbursing yourself from the raffle, asking students to "invest" in the quilt by donating $1 (or some share of the cost) which can then be paid back after the raffle, or inviting a fabric store to be a partner in the project by donating the materials and working with students to assemble the quilt.

Procedure
1. Have each student choose a theme for his or her quilt square. Provide time in the library so students can learn more about their state before deciding. Landmarks, the state bird and flower, significant moments and people in history, state crops and wildlife, and sports teams are possible themes.
2. Provide a sign-up sheet for students to list their choices to avoid duplicating themes.
3. Have students draw and color their designs on squares of paper the same size as the quilt squares, make a few versions, and choose their favorites to transfer to the quilt square.
4. Have students transfer their design to the quilt square using any of a variety of techniques, including fabric markers, fabric paint, fabric crayons, embroidery, puff paints, and applique. They should leave one inch borders around their drawings so that when pieces are sewn together, no designs will be cut off.
5. Sew finished squares together.
6. Tape the back piece of fabric to the floor; lay the quilt-squares piece face down on top; lay the batting down on the back of the quilt-square piece.
7. Sew the three layers together around three edges—two sides and

one end. Turn the entire piece inside out. The batting will now be in the center and the quilt squares piece will be right side up.

7. Baste all three layers together, working from the center to the edges.

8. Hand stitch or machine sew around each square.

9. Plan the details of your raffle. How much will each ticket sell for? When and where will you choose the winning ticket? How will you publicize the event?

10. Donate the proceeds of the raffle to a local food pantry.

Modification

If making a quilt is not feasible, modify the activity by creating calendars that reflect your state. As with the quilt, have each student illustrate themes about your state. Create a template for calendar pages. Have students work in teams to fill in dates to remember each month. Add a page explaining the goal of the project, duplicate all pages, color illustrations, collate, bind with yarn, and sell!

Extension Activities

Language Arts: Create a quilting corner in your classroom. Provide reading materials about quilting, including *The Patchwork Quilt* by Valerie Flourney, illustrated by Jerry Pinkney (Dial Books for Young Readers, 1985); *Tar Beach* by Faith Ringgold (Crown, 1991); *The Quilt Story* by Tony Johnston and Tomie dePaola (Putnam, 1985); and *The Josefina Story* by Eleanor Coerr, illustrated by Bruce Degan (HarperCollins, 1986).

Art: Take quilting to a more personal level with your students by having them create picture quilts of their lives. They might, for example, tell the story of an especially memorable time or event, include an event from each year of their lives, or illustrate their dreams.

Social Studies: Research the prehistoric origins of quilting, then learn more about quilting in Colonial America. Have students draw pictures or write descriptions of what they think certain types of quilts look like, such as crazy quilts and album quilts, then use library resources to find out what they really look like.

Shops For Shelters

Project Goal
To serve meals, and collect canned foods and household items for a shelter.

Project Summary
Geraldine Martin's 1990–1991 first-grade students at L.W. Beecher School in New Haven, Connecticut, opened "Beecher Outlet City," a group of specialty shops, to raise money to make meals for a shelter for homeless and troubled girls. They visited the shelter monthly to make and serve meals, held holiday parties, and corresponded regularly. They won a Kids Care Contest grand prize for their project.

Citizenship Goal
To realize that being a good citizen sometimes takes effort and even hard work, and that the results and positive feelings generated in helping others makes the work worthwhile.

Preparation
Contact a local shelter or group home for children, teens, families, or adults and explain your project goals. If they are able to accept your students' help, talk about the specifics of the project (see Procedure) and set up a schedule of visits when students will prepare, serve, and clean up after meals. Note special days that you would like to celebrate together, such as Thanksgiving. If possible, just to familiarize students and residents with one another, set up a visit to the shelter before students actually prepare and serve a meal for the first time.

Procedure
1. Brainstorm ideas for a class mascot, give it a name, and use this mascot on signs, tags, and posters to identify and advertise shops, products, and activities for the duration of the project (for example, a teddy bear named Buddy Bear).
2. Brainstorm shop ideas. Consider suitability and affordability. Possibilities are:
• Grandma's Attic where you can sell used books and other finds in good condition;
• The Cookie House where students use measuring skills to bake cookies in class to stock their shop (you might ask for family donations to stock this store as well);
• School Stuff for pencils, erasers, rulers, notebook paper, and other school supplies;
• At a shop named after your mascot (Buddy Bear's Baskets), shopping can work in reverse. Place baskets bearing your mascot's picture around the shopping space. Other students can help you help the shelter by donating needed items such as canned food, paper goods, and toiletries.

Shoppers can stop by and drop their donations in the baskets.
3. Begin gathering stock for your school's "Outlet City."
4. Plan the physical space for each shop—can you turn corners of the classroom into shops? Is there a spare room in the school or an area you can "borrow"?
5. Create decorations, signs, and advertisements for each shop.
6. Assign groups of students to staff each shop, rotating shops every 2 to 4 weeks. Students will enjoy taking on the responsibilities of every shop owner—scheduling hours, taking and ordering inventory, organizing, advertising, and banking profits.
7. Use profits from the shops to buy food to make and serve meals at the shelter. Include students and shelter staff in planning menus. Turn shopping for groceries into math activities—estimating total cost, comparing prices, and so on.
8. As holidays arise, plan to bring special celebrations to the shelter with your monthly meal. For example, in November invite shelter residents to your school for a Thanksgiving feast. Plan and prepare a program of songs, skits, and readings. Send shelter residents off with a basket of gifts from your shop of donations.
9. Throughout your participation in this project, correspond with the residents through letters, pictures, and audiotapes.

Modification

If you are unable to visit a shelter on a regular basis to help out, make Friendship Boxes instead. Specify a different type of donation for each week (or month) of your project. Encourage students and staff to bring in whatever is called for that week or month. For example, over a six week period you might collect toothpaste (week 1), shower/bath supplies (week 2), tissues (week 3), socks (week 4), packaged snacks (week 5), and writing/reading materials (week 6). While donations are coming in, gather and decorate shoe boxes with lids. Divide donations among the boxes, add a special message, and deliver to a shelter.

Extension Activities

Language Arts: Read *We Keep a Store* by Anne Shelby (Orchard Books/Franklin Watts, 1990). Ask students what kind of store this family keeps. Brainstorm to come up with all the different kinds of stores people keep. Have students choose one and write their own stories about keeping this kind of store.

Science: Compare the way store items are packaged now to the way they used to be packaged. Challenge students to find out how much packaging their family throws away in one week by setting up a box for this waste. Then challenge them to find ways to buy less packaging.

Modification idea from Nancy Hopfauf's 1990–91 sixth-grade students at Cathedral School in Bismarck, North Dakota.

Stamp Out Drugs

Project Goals
To encourage students to be aware of the many wholesome activities they can be involved in; to encourage students not to use illegal drugs.

Project Summary
Richard Johnson's 1989–90 fifth-grade students at Lakewood Elementary School in Lakewood, New York, campaigned to "stomp out the illegal use of drugs." They created and hung a huge banner filled with activities that they liked to do and placed large footprints on the ceiling from the banner to the hall door. Each student who wanted to join the campaign wrote his or her name on a footprint.

Citizenship Goal
Students will learn about making healthy choices.

Preparation
Choose a motto for your campaign. Decide where footprints will begin and end. Cut out enough footprints to cover that distance.

Procedure
1. Make a large banner with your motto on it.
2. Invite all students "to help stomp out drugs" by writing their names on footprints. Tape these footprints to the ceiling for all to see.

Modification
During Red Ribbon Week (Oct. 22–26), have students wear red ribbons to school as a sign that they want to be drug-free, design "drug-free" T-shirts, hold a rally, or visit younger classes to tell kids not to use drugs.

Extension Activities
Language Arts: Share a book with your class about peer pressure, such as *Earl's Too Cool for Me* by Leah Komaiko (Harper Junior Books/HarperCollins, 1988) or *Chester's Way* by Kevin Henkes (Greenwillow, 1988). Have students write about the last time they had to make a difficult decision.

Art: Students create an anti-drug poster by using their favorite cartoon character. Be sure to write a slogan to go with the character.

Dramatic Arts: Have students role play situations in which they are confronted by someone trying to sell them drugs. Discuss different approaches to handling the situation.

Modification idea from Jeanine Carter's 1990–91 sixth-grade students, Municipal Elementary, Roy, Utah.

Stone Soup

Project Goal
To help feed people at homeless shelters or soup kitchens.

Project Summary
Patricia Miller's 1990–91 fourth-grade students at Clarence Center Elementary School in Clarence Center, New York, organized a cooperative soup-making effort at their school and donated 30 gallons of vegetable soup to a soup kitchen.

Citizenship Goal
To realize that a group of individuals working together can make a significant difference.

Preparation
Read a retelling of the classic French story, *Stone Soup,* retold by Marcia Brown (Macmillan, 1982), to give students an understanding of the story behind their project. Discuss similarities between your project and the story of three soldiers who make soup from stones. Discuss the significance of a single vegetable in helping to feed hungry people. Inform your cafeteria staff of your project and request their cooperation in providing a time and place to cook the soup.

Procedure
1. Have students read several recipes for vegetable soup and choose one, or a combination, to make.
2. Decide how much soup you want to make and calculate the amount of vegetables and other ingredients you'll need.
3. Create a flier inviting students and staff members in your school to take part in your soup project. Include a response form at the bottom (Yes, we will participate; No, we will not participate).
4. Create a second flier for all those participating, specifying donations. For example:
• Primary classes should each provide one bag of barley and one onion;
• Intermediate classes should each provide one can of crushed tomatoes and one onion;
• In addition, individual students/staff members should bring one vegetable, cut up and ready to add to the pot—broccoli, canned corn, potatoes, peas, carrots, green beans, celery.
5. Create a third flier to send home to parents of participating students. Explain the project, provide a space for the child to list the vegetable he or she would like to bring, and give the date it should be brought to school. You might want to take this opportunity to invite parents to school on this day to visit with students and staff as they contribute to the pot.
6. Invite a worker from the soup kitchen to your school on "soup day"

to visit with classes, talk about the organization and the needs of the people it serves, and answer questions.

7. On "soup day," call the classes down one at a time to add ingredients to the pot.

8. Allow soup to cool and package it in jars or large zip-lock style bags before donating it to the soup kitchen.

Modification

You can help a social service organization such as a food pantry without actually cooking food. Adopt a local Meals on Wheels program. Every month, surprise recipients of these meals (many of whom are elderly and homebound) with a special handmade gift. For example, in September, create placemats introducing your class; in October, make fall or Halloween decorations; in November make pinecone turkeys. Continue with a different treat each month. Ask the Meals on Wheels volunteers to distribute the gifts with the meals.

Extension Activities

Language Arts: Follow up "soup day" by having students write and illustrate their own versions of the story *Stone Soup*. Set up a display in the library to share your stories with the rest of the school.

Math: Have students estimate how many people 30 gallons of soup will feed. Provide materials (soup bowls, gallon containers) for testing the estimates.

Social Studies: Obtain estimates of the number of people living at or below poverty level in the United States (use library resources or call a social service agency for more information). Discuss possible reasons people do not have enough money for basic needs such as food. Can students imagine a solution to the problem of hunger in their own community? In the world? Working in teams, have students devise creative solutions to the hunger problem on local, national, and worldwide levels.

4

Environmental Issues

*Projects to clean up the air,
land, and water—
from encouraging the community, to compost,
to testing for acid rain.*

- Coffee Cans for Composting
- Earth Day Every Day
- Energy Check
- Monitoring the Rain
- Operation Paint-the-Town
- Rain Forest Breakfast
- Salt Solutions
- Saving the Earth

Coffee Cans for Composting

Project Goal
To encourage community residents to help solve the solid waste problem by composting organic garbage.

Project Summary
E. Wilhelmina Holden's 1989–90 third-grade students at Marion Street School in Lynbrook, New York, saved more than 100 coffee cans for collecting organic waste, affixed composting labels to all, and wrote a composting information booklet. They distributed composting cans and booklets to community residents and kept in touch to offer encouragement and answer composting questions. They won a Kids Care merit award for their project.

Citizenship Goal
To recognize the importance of community education in changing attitudes and actions.

Preparation
Gather a variety of resources on composting. Have students use them to become familiar with the concept of composting, to identify materials that can and cannot be composted, and to learn the process of composting.

Procedure
1. Decide how many community residents you will distribute composting packs to, and begin collecting that many empty coffee cans (with lids).
2. Design composting labels for cans, including a project logo. Vote on a favorite design, make a copy for each can, and hand color.
3. Have students work in groups to write parts of a composting booklet. Include sections on What Is Composting?, What to Compost, and Ways to Make a Compost Pile.
4. Put all sections together to make a book. Make as many copies as there are cans.
5. Write a pledge for participants to sign: I have looked at the composting information and have discussed it with a class representative. I will consider composting. Signed _____. Ask residents to sign this when they accept the can and booklet.

Extension Activity
Science: If organic waste will decompose in a compost pile, wouldn't it decompose in a landfill just as well? Ask students to design experiments to test their ideas. For example, students might hypothesize that organic garbage in landfills doesn't decompose if it is sealed in plastic bags. To test this, they could bury two similarly-sized apple slices, one wrapped in plastic, the other by itself and observe decomposition of both.

Earth Day Every Day

Project Goal
To increase environmental awareness among students, school staff, and families.

Project Summary
Connie Whitehead Johnson's 1990–91 third-grade students at Mt. Zion Elementary School in Jonesboro, Georgia, made a year-round commitment to protect the environment by setting up paper recycling in their school's classrooms, creating a recycling display to teach others about recycling in the community, sponsoring a Christmas tree recycling drive in December, writing environmental messages to include in the PTA newsletter, participating in a plant-a-tree program, and more. They won a Kids Care Contest merit award for their project.

Citizenship Goal
To recognize education as a way to help solve problems.

Preparation
Since this program is based on recycling, you'll need to research the availability of recycling programs in your community. Find out how recyclable material is transported—do individual centers pick up or do people have to drop off recyclables at the center? Try to make arrangements to have recyclables picked up at your school.

Procedure
1. Set up a recycling display in a high-visibility area of your school—the lobby, library, or cafeteria. Provide information on recycling locations in your area and list procedures for each.
2. Begin an in-school campaign to recycle school paper. First find out how many, if any, classrooms have any kind of recycling system in place. Increase awareness and participation through schoolwide activities:
• write a recycling rap and perform it over the P.A. during morning announcements;
• make educational posters about recycling; and
• write a book for kids about recycling school paper. Include: Why Recycle ("We need to keep our landfills from getting full."), What to Recycle ("When your teacher takes away your paper airplane, unfold it and put it in the recycling box."), and How to Recycle ("Please don't wad up the paper—it takes up too much room.").
3. Research the best way for your school to recycle school paper. One approach is to have a recycling box in each classroom that is periodically emptied into a central bin and then picked up by the recycling facility. Check with your paper recycling center for other suggestions.
4. With the paper-recycling campaign in place, tackle other recycling problems:

- initiate a tree-recycling campaign during the December holidays. Prepare and present public service announcements over the intercom. Make and display posters giving the details;
- learn about the dangers that plastic rings holding six-pack cans present to animals; visit other classrooms to teach students the proper way to cut the rings; sponsor a contest to see which class can bring in the most correctly cut six-pack plastic rings; recycle all of it;
- write environmental messages for school, district, and PTA newsletters. Include tips for recycling, fun facts about recycling, and updates on school recycling progress;
- write fast-food chains encouraging them to use biodegradeable packaging and to set up in-store recycling centers. Find out which ones continue to use polystyrene packaging. Which ones don't?; and
- invite a nursery employee or forester in to help you choose and plant a tree.

Modification

To remind students to sort paper by color or type, decorate three boxes with the kinds of paper that should be put in each—glue scraps of white paper on one, scraps of mixed paper such as colored and construction paper on a second, and scraps of newspaper on a third. Give follow-up presentations to classes who need additional help in separating papers.

Extension Activities

Science: Design and perform a class experiment to find out which decomposes faster—paper made from recycled paper or paper not made from recycled paper.

Language Arts: Invite students' verbal reactions to the following thought starter: Suppose a law was passed requiring all manufacturers to package goods in the same way, without any unnecessary extras. How do you think customers would react? How do you think manufacturers would react?

Art: Create colorful beads from scrap paper. You'll need a variety of paper (magazine pages, white paper, brown paper bags, tissue paper, used envelopes), yarn or string, white glue, scissors, and crayons or markers. Cut paper into long, triangular shapes and roll one at a time around a pencil, starting with the wide end. Glue the tip down and slide the bead off. Use different kinds of paper to create different colors and textures of beads. String beads together to make bracelets or necklaces. Tie them to elastic bands to make hair decorations. Connect many strings of beads together for wall hangings.

Modification idea from Mary Stolze's 1990–91 fourth-grade students at Maple Hills Elementary School in Issaquah, Washington.

Energy Check

Project Goals
To learn to conserve energy and to encourage others to do the same.

Project Summary
Joseph Gravini's 1990–91 fourth-grade students at Ivan G. Smith School in Danvers, Massachusetts, came up with an energy-conservation checklist that they followed for one month. They made an activity and information book about saving energy and shared this with students, staff, and families. They made stuffed eels to block drafts around doors and windows. They gave some to families and friends for holiday gifts and sold others to raise money for their city's Community Council. To remind others to conserve energy, the fourth graders made posters and put them up around their homes and at school.

Preparation
Prepare a lesson on energy conservation. Suggest that students read books about energy, such as *Producing Energy* by Helen H. Carey (Franklin Watts, 1984). Discuss different ways people use energy (for example, turning on a light, using a hair dryer, watching TV, heat). Discuss energy sources—oil, gas, coal, wood, sun. How does each effect the environment? Invite a speaker from your local electric company to talk to your class about energy-saving ideas.

Procedure
1. Create a checklist of ways people can reduce energy consumption, for example, by turning off unused lights and appliances. Make two columns on the checklist—label one "try" and the other "did." Distribute copies to students and have them check which suggestions they will try to improve on over a one-month period. As each of these items is improved upon, have kids check off the "did" column.
2. Create posters to hang up at home and around school as reminders of some of the things on your checklist (to shut off leaky faucets, limit refrigerator openings, air-dry dishes).
3. Put your energy saving ideas into an information book to share with others. Include original games, puzzles, and illustrations.
4. More than half of the energy used at home goes for heat. To prevent some of that heat from being wasted, make draft eels (draft blockers). Have students measure the width of doorways or windows in their homes. Cut material for each draft blocker to measure a couple of inches longer than the width of the door or window and about 10 to 12 inches wide. Each draft blocker requires two pieces this size.
5. Turn the pieces wrong sides out. Sew a seam along both sides and one end. Invert the material and fill with sand. Finish by sewing up the open end. Sew on buttons for eyes.

Modification

Rather than focusing on energy, you could address water conservation. Have students make a list of all the ways they use water. Consult resources such as *Fifty Simple Things Kids Can Do to Save the Earth* by The EarthWorks Group (Andrews and McMeel, 1990) for suggestions on reducing water waste. For example, by turning off the water when you brush your teeth you can save five to seven gallons of water with each brushing. Make a booklet about saving water at school and at home. Share it with students and families.

Extension Activities

Language Arts: Have students write a story about the different ways they saved energy that day. Ask them to underline each verb that shows how the energy was saved. For example: I <u>turned off</u> my kitchen light. Below each underlined word, students should write the type of energy that was saved.

Science: Build a draft finder with a piece of plastic wrap and a stick. Hold the draft detector around window ledges and doors in your home or school to find energy leaks. Devise an energy-conservation plan. Put your plan to use.

Math: On the average, a regular shower head uses six gallons of water per minute. A low-flow shower head uses about half as much water. Estimate how much water your family could save if they installed a low-flow shower head. To do this, write down approximately how many minutes each person in your household spends in the shower in one day. Total up the time. Multiply this number by six to get the number of gallons of water used. Divide this number in half. This number is the amount of water your family could save each day if you installed a low-flow shower head.

Dramatic Arts: Ask students to act out different ways that they use energy (doing laundry, making toast). Discuss appliances that are human-powered and those that need other sources of energy.

Monitoring the Rain

Project Goals
To measure the amount of acid rain in an area; to become aware of the dangers of acid rain.

Project Summary
Mary Treacy, Chris Armstrong, and Kathy Mazzarelli's 1990–91 sixth-grade students at Highland Falls Middle School in Highland Falls, New York, and Carol DeGroot's 1990–91 fifth-grade students at Pioneer School in Green Bay, Wisconsin, tested for acid rain in their communities. Every day for six weeks, the students collected rain and measured its acidity level with a specially designed kit. They also monitored the weather, the wind direction, and sky conditions. They recorded their findings on a special computer card, tabulated and mapped data to show the current acid rain situation in North America, and shared their results with their communities.

Citizenship Goal
To learn that the world does not consist of isolated towns—we are part of a much larger community that needs attention and care.

Preparation
Acid rain is considered a pollutant of both water and air. Discuss some of the causes of acid rain, including car exhaust and factory smokestacks. Discuss what acid rain consists of, where it is found, what effects it has on the environment, and what we can do to control the problem. Have students test for acid rain in your community. Order an acid-rain testing kit (see Resources) or set up an experiment on your own.

Procedure
1. After learning about acid rain, set up a jar or test tube in an area outside your school where no one will disturb it.
2. Each day, check the jar to see if any liquid has collected in it.
3. If the jar is empty, have students rinse it with distilled water and return it outside. If it has rained, and the jar is still empty, you may want to put a funnel in the mouth of the jar.
4. If the jar has liquid in it, test it with a PH strip or litmus paper to determine if it is acidic, alkaline, or neutral. If water tested with blue litmus turns red, then the water is acidic. If water tested with red litmus turns blue, the water is alkaline. If no changes occur when both litmus papers are tested, the water is neutral.
5. Record your results each day that you test rain water. Is there a problem with acid rain where you live? What do you think some causes of acid rain are in your community?
6. Write letters of concern to senators and state representatives. Include a list of suggestions on ways to help control acid rain.

Modification

In areas where there is little or no rainfall, have students test the acidity levels of streams, ponds, lakes, fountains, or sink water. Collect samples in small clean jars. Label each jar by writing down the location where the water sample was collected. Test each water sample with a strip of red and blue litmus paper. Have students record their results. Were any of the water sources acidic? What effect does acidic water have on plant and animal life?

Extension Activities

Science: Acid rain can be carried from one area to another by the wind. Have students study a weather map to see the direction of winds across the United States. Using the map, determine where acid rain produced by industrial pollution in the northwest could end up. Show the movement of acid rain across the country.

Language Arts: Read *Just a Dream* by Chris Van Allsburg (Houghton Mifflin, 1990), in which the protagonist has a nightmare about a world ruined by people's careless treatment of the environment. Have students write their own "Just a Dream" stories, approaching the subject from a different angle. In their stories, have students write about dreams in which they predict positive changes in the environment.

Science: Have students spread petroleum jelly on the inside of four clean, clear jars. Students should then place the jars in four different locations outdoors. After a week, bring the jars back inside. Did students find anything stuck inside their jars? Have them report and discuss their findings.

Art: Have students paint a mural depicting what they think the earth might look like in 100 years if we don't stop polluting our air, land, and water. Then have students brainstorm a list of steps they can take to prevent the earth from looking like their mural.

Operation Paint-the-Town

Project Goal
To encourage members of the community not to litter.

Project Summary
Suellen Hansen's 1989–90 fifth-grade students at Unquowa School in Fairfield, Connecticut, decorated trash barrels, placed them throughout their community, and spent a day picking up trash.

Citizenship Goal
To recognize that setting a good example can make positive changes.

Preparation
Contact your public works department or local businesses and organizations for trash barrel and paint donations. Map out where each painted barrel will be placed.

Procedure
1. Paint a base coat on each barrel.
2. Sketch out designs on paper that you would like to paint on the barrels, for example, your school or community emblem or mascot.
3. Draw those designs on the barrels with washable markers. Trace over them with permanent markers.
4. Paint over your design with enamel paint. Allow to dry.
5. Distribute each barrel to its designated place.
6. Spend a day picking up trash to show your community you care about keeping it clean.

Modification
Arrange for students to remove graffiti from a building or bridge that has been defaced. If the graffiti cannot be removed, make arrangements for students to paint over the graffiti.

Extension Activities
Language Arts: Write public-service announcements to encourage people to keep your city litter free. Deliver them during morning announcements and send copies to local newspapers, and radio and TV stations.

Math: Spend a day picking up trash around your school. Weigh each bag of trash that is collected. Total the weight of all bags collected. If the same amount of litter was collected each day for a month, how many pounds of litter would there be? After one year?

Rain Forest Breakfast

Project Goals

To raise awareness of the importance of preserving rain forests and to earn money to purchase and protect rain forest land.

Project Summary

Jan Fremont's 1989–90 fifth-grade students at Daniel Boone Elementary School in Wentzville, Missouri, sponsored a community rain forest breakfast, serving foods that come from rain forest crops. They raised money to buy the food by starting a business and issuing stock for 25 cents a share. They used proceeds from the breakfast to purchase 18 acres of rain forest.

Citizenship Goal

To understand the interdependency of living things and our responsibilities toward them, including those beyond our own nation.

Preparation

A study of rain forests and the interdependence of organisms will help students acquire the knowledge and understanding they need to appreciate this project and their success. Clear the idea of setting up a company and selling stock with your building administrator. Make arrangements with cafeteria staff to use refrigerators, freezers, utensils, bowls, and so on.

Procedure

1. Form a company to obtain money to buy ingredients for your breakfast. Give your company a name and elect a board of directors.
2. Set up various committees to direct different parts of the project:
• the executive committee plans the date, time, place, and cost per person of the breakfast;
• the board of directors designs stock certificates and writes breakfast invitations that include response forms;
• the information committee organizes rain forest presentations for other classes. Presentors can share stories about rain forests [for example, *The Crocodile and the Crane: Surviving in a Crowded World* by Judy Cutchins and Ginny Johnston (Morrow, 1986) or *The Great Kapok Tree* by Lynne Cherry (Gulliver/Harcourt Brace Jovanovich, 1990), and explain the company, the concept of selling shares, and the breakfast. Before concluding, presentors should distribute invitations to students and request that they share them with their families and return all response forms with money by a certain date;
• the advertising committee designs and displays posters, fliers, banners, and other material about the breakfast;
• the board of directors sells the stock, keeping accurate records of who buys how many shares;

- the financial committee keeps running records of shares, breakfast tickets sold, and to whom they were sold;
- the chefs committee plans the menu, researching rain forest crops (such as chocolate, pineapple, coffee, rice, bananas, oranges, coconut, nuts, and corn), offering suggestions to the class, and taking a vote on the final menu; and
- decorators direct students in making decorations (placemats, centerpieces, murals).

3. Shop for breakfast ingredients several days before the breakfast.
4. Two to three days before the breakfast, begin preparing food. Prepare drinks such as hot chocolate and coffee the day of the breakfast.
5. Prepare a display of rain forest information for breakfast patrons.
6. Arrive early the day of the breakfast. Set up decorations, tables, serving centers, and information displays. Assign jobs to all students (serving, cleaning tables, staffing information displays, and cleaning up when breakfast is over).
7. Before breakfast is over, compute total proceeds (after deducting cost of food and shares/dividends to be paid) and announce how many acres of rain forest students will purchase.
8. Return initial investments and dividends. Send proceeds to the organization of your choice.

Modification

There are many ways to raise money to purchase rain forest land. Start an aluminum can recycling bin in your lunchroom. Capture students' attention to the project by decorating the recycling bin to resemble a giant soda can. Post an explanation of the project nearby to generate interest.

Extension Activities

Art/Science: Provide scrap construction paper, newspaper, straws, toothpicks, colored pencils and crayons, and other art supplies. Challenge students to create new species of birds indigenous to the rain forest, keeping in mind how different layers of the rain forest are specialized for various needs, such as eating. Have students name their birds, write fact cards about the new species, and create a bulletin board display with their work.

Social Studies/Math: Survey local fast-food restaurants to find out where the cattle their beef comes from is raised. How much of the cattle is raised on land once occupied by tropical rain forests? Have students compare the cost per ounce of hamburgers from various chains. Can they draw any conclusions about the price of a hamburger and the origin of the beef?

Modification idea from Helene Hinck (student council advisor) and the 1990–91 second-grade student council at Riker Hill Elementary in Livingston, New Jersey.

Salt Solutions

Project Goal
To convince cities to reduce salt use as a road deicing agent and to recommend more environmentally sound alternatives.

Project Summary
Cathlynn Brusky's 1990–91 sixth-grade students at Madison Junior High School in Appleton, Wisconsin, conducted research and performed experiments to learn more about the effects of salt on the environment. They sent a survey about salt use to the directors of public works in 50 cities throughout their state. They investigated the financial angle of different deicing policies, presented their findings to local officials, and succeeded in changing the town's winter salting policy. These students won a Kids Care Contest merit award for their project.

Citizenship Goal
To learn that children's voices and opinions are valued.

Preparation
Find out about your area's winter salting policy—what is the policy and who is responsible for determining it? (It may be a street and sanitation committee or the department of public works.) If it involves salting, investigate the effects of salt on the environment (slows seed germination; kills plants; contaminates groundwater; reacts chemically with heavy metals, such as those used in cars, to produce dangerous chemicals; causes soil to erode more quickly; disturbs the algae level in lakes; and harms fish and other aquatic life).

Procedure
1. Write a survey to learn about the deicing policies of other cities in your state. Questions should address the types of deicers used, the number of pounds used per lane mile, the cost and amount used per year, type of deicer storage facility, and the number of miles of roads in that city. Ask how the city's deicing policy was established. You might ask for assistance from a marketing firm or a high school or university marketing instructor in developing the survey.
2. Address your surveys to the director of public works in each of your state's cities.
3. While waiting for survey responses, gather additional information:
• design and carry out an experiment to test the effects of salt on seed germination and plant growth;
• invite the supervisor of your area's water quality control board to share information about water quality control in your community;
• invite the director of public works or the street supervisor in to talk about the history of your community's deicing policies, the number of miles of road now serviced, and the cost of materials for deicing these

roads each year; and
- invite a local public official to talk about how policy changes are made.

4. As survey responses come in, chart the results. Summarize the findings in a report. Send a copy to each participant.

5. Use information from the surveys to research alternate deicing agents. For example, you might find that a 100 percent salt usage policy is substantially more expensive than sand or a mix of salt and stone chips. Chart this information as it applies to your city.

6. If students determine that a more environmentally sound solution to deicing exists for their community, have them request an appointment with those responsible for making the deicing policy. Go armed with results from the statewide survey, graphs and charts showing cost savings, environmental data, recommendations for a revised policy (including information from other cities about what works), and copies of all to share.

Modification

In areas where deicing is not an issue, you can take a similar approach to do something about other environmentally harmful practices in your community. Research the use of lawn pesticides, their effects on the environment, and alternative lawn-care solutions. Survey community members about their use of pesticides and create a campaign to institute more environmentally sound lawn-care policies.

Extension Activities

Science: Have students design experiments to test their own deicing solutions, measuring the success of alternative deicers by testing them against salt on similarly-sized ice cubes.

Geography: Display a large world map and ask students to write down the five countries they think produce the most salt. Next have them guess which industry consumes the most salt. Finally, have them consult library resources to find the correct answers. Discuss reasoning behind their original answers and how they compare with actual answers.

Math: What geometric shape do salt crystals most closely resemble? Have students use magnifying glasses to see salt formations and consult their math books or an upper-grade book to find the answer. What other common substances have similarly shaped particles?

Social Studies: Compose student panels of five each, assigning students in each group the parts of an environmentalist, a salt manufacturer, a salt miner, a concerned citizen, and the governor of a leading salt-producing state. Knowing that about 20 percent of the salt consumed in the United States is used for deicing roads, have them react to the following question: How do you feel about cities and towns now using 100 percent salt deicing programs adopting alternative policies that use significantly less salt?

Saving the Earth

Project Goal
To increase awareness of the importance of recycling and conserving.

Project Summary
Each week, students in Moylene Davis's 1990–91 second-grade class at Goodwell Elementary in Goodwell, Oklahoma, cleaned up a certain area near their school. They recycled the cans and glass that they found. They informed the school staff, other students, and community members of the importance of recycling and conserving.

Citizenship Goal
To learn that what kids do now can make a difference in their world tomorrow.

Preparation
Organize clean-up patrol teams for different areas around your school. For example, one team might be in charge of the playground and another the front lawn. Set aside a time each week when teams will clean up their designated areas. Before you begin, have students bring in used paper bags for collecting garbage. Set up labeled bins to collect each kind of garbage you will recycle (paper, glass, aluminum). Decide when and how the recyclable materials will get to the appropriate center. Try to arrange for the materials to be picked up, or for parents to drop them off.

Procedure
1. At the designated time each week, clean-up patrol teams tackle their assigned areas. To facilitate sorting of recyclable garbage, have one student on a team collect all the glass garbage, another all the aluminum, and so on.
2. After they've cleaned up their area, have students place recyclable garbage in the appropriate bins.
3. Have kids collaborate to write an article for their school paper urging everyone to recycle and conserve energy.
4. Together with your students, create a poster campaign telling others around school and town what they can do to save the earth.

Modifications
- If cleaning up once a week is too much for one grade level, make it a schoolwide project. Assign one class from each grade level to clean up a particular area.
- Have students organize a "Clean Sweep Day." Invite everyone in the community to help pick up litter from roadsides, yards, parks, beaches, and so on. Ask your PTA or a local grocery store to donate the bags. Put up posters and make announcements over the school P.A. system to

alert everyone to this upcoming day. Set up a garbage bag pick-up and drop-off point. Divide participants into groups, each responsible for a certain area of the community.

• Adopt a two-mile stretch of a highway. Several times a year, clean up both sides of the highway ditches. Recycle any cans and glass that you find.

Extension Activities

Language Arts: Have students practice their letter-writing skills by writing persuasive letters to local companies, businesses, universities, and other schools explaining the importance of recycling. Include easy suggestions for recycling. Write congratulatory letters to those with positive environmental practices.

Art: Design "Save the Earth" T-shirts. Each time students meet to clean up their assigned areas, they can wear them to show everyone they are trying to make the earth a better place.

Math: For every 100 bottles you recycle, you save a gallon of gasoline. Calculate approximately how many glass bottles your family throws away each week. How many gallons of gasoline could your family save each week? In a year?

Modification ideas from Grace Alder Foxwell's 1990–91 second-grade students, Pinehurst Elementary, Salisbury, Maryland; Annette Adams's 1989–90 fifth-grade students, Tuckers Crossroads, Lebanon, Tennessee; Sandra Renner's 1990–91 third- and fourth-grade students, Pollack Grade School, Pollack, South Dakota.

5

Animal Protection

*Projects to protect animals—
from organizing a pet-food drive for abused and
unwanted animals to stopping the
slaughter of dolphins.*

Adopt a Sea Lion

Bird Buddies

Elephants Alive

Kids Give a Hoot

Letters for Marine Life

Pet Friends

Whale World

Adopt a Sea Lion

Project Goals
To increase awareness of ecological causes and to protect sea life.

Project Summary
Nancy Dykema Neilsont and the 1988–89 kindergarten through fourth-grade students at McDowell Elementary School in Laguna Niguel, California, recycled cans and glass to support two blind sea lions at the Friends of the Sea Lion Marine Mammal Center in Laguna Beach, California.

Citizenship Goal
To learn about the importance of taking care of living things.

Preparation
Set up recycling containers at your school. Research organizations that care for and protect sea life. Choose one to receive proceeds of your recycling campaign. Set up a notebook to keep an ongoing record of cans and bottles recycled and money earned.

Procedure
1. Have students design fliers encouraging families, neighbors, and other community members to participate in the recycling project.
2. Keep a running total of money received for recyclable materials.
3. Once you've reached your goal, present the money to your cause.

Modification
There are a variety of different animals that can be "adopted" (check resource page for listings). Another way kids can care for animals is to volunteer at the A.S.P.C.A. to help wash, walk, or clean animals.

Extension Activities
Language Arts: Encourage students to make every day Earth Day by trying this project: Divide the class into small groups. Assign each group a month of the year. Have kids make up a calendar grid for their month. Then have students research and brainstorm ecology facts, recycling tips, and other earth-keeping advice. Students should then try to fill each day on the grid with a fact, tip, or message. Encourage them to relate information to their specified month (for example, for the end of December: "Don't forget to recycle your Christmas tree."). Compile grids to make an ecology calendar.

Art: Have students brainstorm a list of sea animals, look for pictures of these animals in books, and make papier-maché replicas of different kinds of sea creatures, such as sharks, whales, dolphins, and sea turtles.

Bird Buddies

Project Goal
To increase the vanishing Eastern Bluebird population.

Project Summary
Diane McCarron's 1989–90 fourth-grade students at Hagan School in Poughkeepsie, New York, built nesting boxes designed especially for bluebirds, and created a bluebird trail in their community to encourage the population growth of this species.

Citizenship Goal
To learn that successful projects often involve the support of many, and that obstacles can be overcome by working together.

Preparation
Contact a local bird-watching group, an ornithologist at a nearby university, or a 4-H club for information about building, placing, monitoring, and maintaining bluebird houses (see Resources).

Procedure
1. Learn more about the comeback of the bluebird, native only to North America. When and where does it nest? How can proper design of a nesting box prevent other birds from taking over? What do bluebirds like to eat? Do they migrate?
2. Obtain plans for building a bluebird house. Make a list of materials, costs, and basic construction steps.
3. Raise money for your materials by recycling cans and bottles.
4. Invite district industrial arts teachers to offer building tips and assist students in cutting wood.
5. After assembling bluebird boxes, invite parents and interested community members to help prepare the trail and place the boxes.
6. Make regular visits to the bluebird trail to monitor and maintain the boxes. Keep a journal of your visits.

Modifications
The bluebird, New York's state bird, was once faced with declining numbers. It's making a comeback thanks to people who build and maintain special nesting boxes for them. Bluebirds can be found in other parts of the country as well as New York State, so even if you're located in another state, you may still be able to participate in this project. Check with a local bird watch group to find out if the bluebird population can be encouraged in your area.

If not, choose a bird common to your area that would benefit from special attention. Proceed with the project as described, substituting the proper kind of care as indicated by experts.

Extension Activities

Science: Turn a bird walk into a scavenger hunt. Have students look for 1) birds hopping; 2) birds eating; 3) birds on a utility wire; 4) birds cleaning their feathers; 5) birds feeding their young; 6) birds with more than one color; 7) birds with differently shaped beaks; 8) birds gliding; 9) birds singing; 10) birds building nests.

Creative Arts: If students were birds, what kinds of homes would protect them and provide the best shelter? Have them design their ideal homes, reflecting specific needs such as keeping out other kinds of birds and animals that might threaten their survival.

Math: Take a bird census. Together, name five to ten favorite birds, including your state bird. Find out how many of each existed fifty years ago. Twenty-five years ago? Ten years ago? Five years ago? Now? Have students graph information, then add an additional bar—based on what they've learned, have students predict each bird's population five years from now.

Elephants Alive

Project Goal
To increase awareness of the plight of elephants and to help save them from extinction.

Project Summary
Sande Zirlin, Bill Blance, and their 1989–90 fifth-grade students at William H. Barkley Elementary School in Amsterdam, New York, created a giant mural showing a great herd of elephants safe from poachers and harm; they sent a photograph of the mural, together with a letter expressing their concerns, to government leaders and environmental organizations.

Citizenship Goal
To learn that individuals working as a group can help bring about increased awareness and change.

Preparation
Discuss the killing of elephants for their tusks. Identify objects made from ivory, such as jewelry and statues. Research elephants and their habitats.

Procedure
1. Sketch a plan of your mural. Include elements of the African plains such as grasslands, water holes, mountains, elephants, and other native animals and plants.
2. On individual pieces of paper, have each student paint an elephant and cut it out.
3. Brainstorm a slogan for your save-the-elephants campaign. Paint that at the top of the mural.
4. Transfer your sketch to the mural paper.
5. Once the background is complete, paste the elephants in place. Hang the mural in a well-trafficked area of the school.
6. Have students compose a letter expressing their concerns about Africa's elephants. Identify ways other people can help stop the killing before elephants become extinct. Invite others in your school to sign the letter.
7. Send the letter, together with a photo of your mural, to as many influential people as possible; for example, the president of the United States, your mayor, your governor, the United Nations, the presidents of African nations where poaching occurs, and conservation groups.

Modification
To increase children's awareness of endangered animals, sponsor an endangered-animal parade. Have each student create a mask to

represent an endangered animal. Set aside a day and time to parade through the school.

Extension Activities

Art: Design a bookmark about elephants. Include your save-the-elephant logo. Cover your bookmark with contact paper. Give them out to students at your school to create more awareness of the slaughtering of African elephants.

Language Arts: Read *The Elephant's Child* by Rudyard Kipling (Macmillan, 1972). Then have students write and illustrate their own "Just So" story about how the elephant got its trunk.

Social Studies: Have students find out what other animals are threatened or endangered by writing to the World Wildlife Fund (see Resources). Have each student research an animal and the efforts that are being made to protect it. Illustrate, alphabetize, and compile the entries to make a dictionary on endangered and threatened animals.

Math: Have students research statistics on the declining elephant population in African countries and use the figures to create a bar graph. Students may also want to translate the statistics into a picture graph to display on a bulletin board in the hallway. Have students devise a key that shows what a picture of one elephant represents (each picture might stand for 1,000 elephants).

Social Studies: Encourage students to start their own wildlife club. Students can send a self-addressed, stamped envelope to Friends of Wildlife (see Resources) along with a letter requesting information about the group's adopted elephant herd and tips for starting their own club.

Kids Give a Hoot

Project Goals
To become aware of the role birds of prey play in the environment; to protect them by adopting a bird of prey.

Project Summary
Janet Willmann's 1990–91 second-grade students at Mesnier Elementary School in Affton, Missouri, researched and studied birds of prey, focusing on the owls of Missouri. They collected aluminum cans and used the proceeds to adopt an owl.

Citizenship Goal
To learn that through caring and education, students can help improve their environment.

Preparation
Prepare class lessons and discussions to help students learn about birds of prey. Describe characteristics of a bird of prey (silent flight, keen eyesight, talons, acute hearing, and curved beak for ripping or tearing prey). Make sure kids understand the difference between endangered and extinct with regard to the animal kingdom. Arrange for a ranger or ornithologist to guide your class through a park or bird watching area (preferably a place where birds of prey are known to live). Or visit a local raptor (bird of prey) rehabilitation center.

Procedure
1. As a class, begin a bird-watching log. The log will be used to document where a bird was seen, its song or call (if known), the date and time of day, and anything else the student might want to include, such as a sketch.
2. Set up an aluminum-can recycling center in your class or school.
3. Each week, bring the cans to a recycling site. Use the proceeds to "adopt" a bird of prey from a Raptor Rehabilitation and Propagation organization.

Modification
Other animals besides birds of prey can be "adopted" for this project (see Resources). Money for "adopting" an animal can be earned by any fund-raising project. For example, have students design and sell T-shirts depicting the animal they wish to "adopt."

Extension Activities
Art: Cut out silhouettes of owls; use them to construct owl mobiles to hang in the classroom.

Language Arts: Read a story about a bird of prey, such as *Moths &*

Mothers, Feathers & Fathers by Barry Shles (Jalmar Press, 1989), the story of a tiny owl that cannot fly. Have students write their own stories. If they could fly, where would they go?

Science: Help provide food for birds in the winter by building bird feeders. Make a simple one by cutting out one side of a milk carton. Insert a thin wooden dowel or twig lengthwise across the open side of the carton to give birds something to stand on. Fill the bottom with seeds and berries. Hang it from a tree.

Geography: Make a list of places throughout the United States where the particular bird of prey you are studying is found. Locate and mark these places on a U.S. map.

Math: Find out how many different kinds of owls there are. Make a graph to show how many of each are alive today. Are any endangered? What could you do to help?

Social Studies: The spotted owl is becoming quite rare. They live in forests that are being cut down for paper and lumber products. Environmentalists are trying to get the loggers to stop cutting down the trees, but loggers argue that this is the way they make their livings. Divide the class into two sides. Have one side argue for the loggers and the other side for preserving the owls.

Letters for Marine Life

Project Goal
To help stop the slaughter of dolphins.

Project Summary
Gerri Faivre's 1989–90 fifth-grade students at East Woods School in Oyster Bay, New York, organized an extensive letter-writing campaign to raise awareness about the killing of dolphins in tuna nets, petitioned government leaders to protect dolphins, and requested that school food service organizations use dolphin-safe tuna or serve alternative choices.

Citizenship Goal
To recognize that sharing information about problems is a powerful tool for effecting change.

Preparation
Gather information from a variety of sources about the dolphin/tuna issue. Try to get information reflecting several viewpoints, including those of marine environmentalists and of commercial fisheries (see Resources). Students should be well informed before beginning their campaign to end the killing of dolphins.

Procedure
1. Develop a fact sheet on dolphins (include easy-to-understand explanations of related terms such as *driftnetting* and *purse-seining*) and a list of suggestions for taking action to protect dolphins.
2. Make a list of government officials, environmentalists, commercial fisheries still using nets to catch tuna, companies canning dolphin-unsafe tuna, restaurants that serve tuna, stores that sell tuna, school food services, and others who you feel could benefit from your information and would take action to support your cause.
3. Decide on the best approach for addressing each person, organization, and business on your list. For example, if students are writing restaurants that serve tuna, they might want to share information about the plight of dolphins, identify both companies that market tuna that is dolphin-unsafe and those that sell only dolphin-safe tuna, and thank them if they are already buying from companies that use only dolphin-safe tuna. If students are writing a member of Congress, they might want to ask what the individual's position is on this issue and request information about actions this person is taking or plans to take. Include the fact sheet and action list with all letters sent.
4. Draft a petition and a letter explaining the dolphin/tuna issue and the reasoning behind the petition (what you hope to accomplish, who is being invited to sign it, who it will be delivered to). Distribute dolphin fact sheets as you ask students and staff in your school and other schools to sign the petition.

5. Create a forum for sharing results and responses with other members of your school community, for example a class newsletter or a bulletin board in the library or school lobby.

Modification

Joining an organization is another way to help protect marine animals. Raise money through a recycling campaign to join a group such as Earth Island Institute (see Resources). Read it for updates, then spread the word by sharing it with another class.

Extension Activities

Consumer Studies: Have students study canned tuna labels. Which ones say "dolphin-safe?" Is there information on the label that supports this claim? Have students write to companies making this claim. Ask for information that backs up the claim. Compare it with information from Earth Island Institute. Do they agree? If not, discuss reasons for the discrepancies. Next, have students study labels of various types of tuna canned by the same company. If one type says "dolphin-safe," but another doesn't, would students buy either? Why or why not?

Social Studies: Track the progress of bills introduced in Congress to protect dolphins and other sea animals from being killed in drift nets. Find out where your representative stands on these issues.

Math: How much is a million? That's about how many sea animals are killed each year in driftnets used to catch tuna. Help students better visualize this number with the following activities: How many rolls of pennies would equal 1 million pennies? (answer: 20,000) How many years does it take to make 1 million days? (answer: about 2,740) How many schools like yours would it take to equal 1 million kids? (answers will vary).

Pet Friends

Project Goal
To collect cat and dog food for abused and unwanted animals.

Project Summary
Lori Jones, Lynn Robertson, Kim Moretz, and special education students at Emma Havens Young School in Brick, New Jersey, organized a different kind of canned-food drive—one for cats and dogs. Their donations helped feed animals at a zoo for injured and abandoned animals.

Citizenship Goal
To make students aware of the responsibilities of pet ownership and of the need to care for all living things.

Preparation
Before introducing this project, determine that an outlet for distributing dog and cat food to needy animals exists. For example, in Brick, New Jersey, the Popcorn Park Zoo is devoted to rescuing and caring for unwanted and abused animals. Call your local humane society for more information.

Procedure
1. Create posters and displays to inform the school about your project. State goals and dates to remember (start of food drive, days food will be picked up, and so on).
2. Have students prepare presentations to share with other classrooms. They should tell how they became interested in the project, why it is important, and how other kids can help. Students might include graphs showing the number of cats, dogs, and other animals that are abused and unwanted, and how much of each kind of food the animal shelter needs each month.
3. Hold a schoolwide contest challenging each class to design the best food-collection container and collect the most food.
4. At the close of the food drive, hold an awards ceremony announcing winners in the different categories and the total amount of food collected. Invite a representative from the shelter to speak about pet care and accept your donation.

Modifications
• If your area lacks a shelter or organization that cares for unwanted and abused animals, you can help by working to educate others about caring for animals. First, take a school survey to find out the kinds of animals people own. Generate giant graphs showing different kinds of information: How many of each kind of animal is owned? What

percentage of the people surveyed own pets? Next, research needs and proper care for each of these animals. Display graphs and results of research in the school library, lobby, or other common space.
• Organize a contest challenging students or classes to create the best poster about responsible pet care. Display winning posters in the public library, stores, banks, and other prominent places in the community.

Extension Activities

Social Studies: Ask children to guess what kinds of pets people have in other countries. Would they believe mongooses, cormorants, even penguins? Learn more about common pets in other countries. What makes a good home for these pets? How are they cared for?

Math/Science: Make a healthy treat to share with the dogs owned by students and staff in your school. Here's how:

Dog Treats
(adapted from Applehood and Motherpie; RJL Publications)
Ingredients: 1¾ cups flour; 1 cup whole wheat flour; ½ cup rye flour; 1 cup unprocessed wheat; ½ cup corn meal; ¼ cup instant non-fat dry milk; 1½ tablespoons salt; ½ envelope dry yeast; ½ teaspoon beef bouillon powder; 2 tablespoons hot water; 1 egg, beaten with 1 tablespoon milk; 1¾ cups chicken broth.
Directions: 1) Combine first seven ingredients. 2) In a separate bowl, dissolve yeast in bouillon. Stir in egg mixture. 3) Add enough broth to make a stiff dough. 4) Roll dough on a floured surface to ⅛-inch thickness. Cut into shapes. 5) Place on greased cookie sheets and bake at 300° until edges are brown (about 40 minutes). 6) Turn oven off. Leave biscuits in oven overnight.

Language Arts: Have kids take the point of view of an abandoned pet and create a flier or newspaper advertisement seeking adoption. Students should include a picture (can be drawn or cut from a magazine), a description, information about the kind of home and owner desired, and a list of the needs a new owner must meet.

Whale World

Project Goal
To help students become aware of the need to protect the environment.

Project Summary
Elizabeth Rudinsky's 1990–91 third-grade students at P.S. 40 in New York City, conducted an in-depth study of whales and their environment. They organized activities to educate others about whales and raised money for whale research.

Citizenship Goal
To recognize that students not only have to become aware of global issues but also that they are responsible for doing something to bring about positive change.

Preparation
This project has the potential to last all year. Decide how much time you can devote to the project and select as many elements as you feel you can incorporate. Consider tying in the entire project across your curriculum as a theme-based unit.

Procedure
1. Begin by learning more about whales and the problems facing some kinds of whales. Study the cultures of countries where people once hunted or still hunt whales to try and understand their reasons for killing them.
2. Outline a schedule of short- and long-term activities and events, including a schoolwide presentation about whales and a fund-raising event for an organization that protects sea life.
3. Invite a marine biologist or a representative from an organization involved in protecting whales (see Resources) to speak with students about whales.
4. As students gain the knowledge they need to address other people about the preservation of whales, have them write letters to officials in places where people still hunt whales, asking them to discontinue the practice.
5. Set up a display in your school to educate others about the need to protect whales. Include student reports, copies of letters sent to officials and their replies, recommended readings for students and staff who want to learn more, a map showing where different kinds of whales can be found and where they are still hunted. Post a calendar of upcoming events that your class has planned.
6. Organize a fund-raiser to raise money to help save whales. Donate the proceeds to an organization that can help.
7. Write, produce, and perform a schoolwide dramatic presentation about whales to share students' knowledge with the rest of the school

community. For example, you might dramatize the act of whaling, with students playing the roles of hunters, whale product processors, and people who want to protect whales. Show hunting and processing techniques, incorporate education against the practice, and provide information about the future of whales. Make the price of admission a small donation to the organization you identified or a letter written to an appropriate official asking that whaling be discontinued.

Modification

Depending on where your school is located, your students might prefer to focus on an animal closer to home. For example, students living in or near Florida might want to organize activities and events to support the manatee, a sea mammal found in Florida's bays and rivers, and hunted for its hide, flesh, and oil.

Extension Activities

Language Arts/Science: Hold a whale scavenger hunt. List distinguishing characteristics of different kinds of whales. (There are more than 75.) Challenge students to identify each whale by name within a given amount of time.

Math: Bring the biggest whale to your school grounds. Start with a 12-inch-long drawing of a blue whale copied from a photograph. Place tissue or tracing paper marked off in 1-inch grids over the photograph. Grid by grid, transfer the image to a second, larger piece of paper marked in 8-foot grids. Designate a section of your playground for your life-size "drawing." Mark 1-foot grids on the grass or pavement with chalk. Transfer the images in each grid of the smaller drawing to each grid of the outdoor drawing.

If your drawing is on pavement, request permission to make the whale permanent with paint. If the whale is on grass, ask custodians to mow around the original chalk outline and continue to do so each time they mow the grass. Your whale will take on its shape as grass within the outline grows.

Science: Whales in the Antarctic feed mainly on crustaceans called krill. As the human population grows, krill is being considered as a possible food source for people. Ask students to imagine that more and more people are fishing for krill. Have them predict and list the chain of events that might follow.

6

Global Awareness

Projects to increase awareness of the world as everyone's community—from promoting worldwide literacy to welcoming new immigrants.

Book Relief

Books for the World

Care Packages

Children to Children

Paper Cranes for Peace

Trees for Ireland

Book Relief

Project Goal
To support the cause of worldwide literacy.

Project Summary
Susan Melenric's 1990–91 fourth-grade students at First Ward Elementary School in Morgantown, West Virginia, learned that books are not available to many children in third-world countries. They raised money through a variety of activities to help establish a library in a Guatemalan orphanage where there previously were no reading materials. They continue to maintain and expand the library through an on-going fund-raising campaign.

Citizenship Goal
To recognize global responsibilities as part of being a good citizen.

Preparation
Contact Bibliotecas (see Resources), an organization that establishes libraries in Central America, to determine how your class can best make a contribution. For example, for a certain amount of money, you can establish a library. By continuing to raise money each year, you'll maintain and expand this library. Or, you can raise money to donate any number of books that will be used to either expand existing libraries or, along with other donations, help start up a new library.

Procedure
Use Bibliotecas' theme, *All the flowers of all the tomorrows are in the seeds of today*, to plan a schoolwide campaign to raise money for the organization:

1. In the school lobby or library, display and label a five-foot flower stem for each grade. For a 25 cent contribution (or any amount you choose), a donor can buy a petal for his or her grade's flower—flattened cupcake holders work well for petals. After purchasing petals, students write their names on the petals and glue them to their grade's flower. Decide how students and staff members can go about making donations—you might identify specific times during the day when contributions will be accepted, such as before school and during lunch.

2. Send teams of students to each classroom to share information about the project and explain the flower system.

3. During your fund-raising campaign, make time to design bookplates for the books your class helps purchase. Sponsor a contest for the best bookplate design. Photocopy the winning design and have students decorate and write a message on each bookplate.

4. Create bookmarks for children at the orphanage where your books will be delivered.

5. When you've reached your goal, send a check, the bookplates, and the bookmarks to Bibliotecas.

6. Follow up with letters and drawings to your new friends at the orphanage.

Modification

You can help children in third-world countries with other needs, too. One way to do so is to sponsor a child through an organization that provides meals, housing, education, and medical care to children who lack adequate care. The Resources section lists several such organizations. Monthly sponsorships generally run between $12 and $30. You'll receive information about the child you're sponsoring and have opportunities to correspond with him or her through the organization you choose.

Extension Activities

Language Arts: Invite a member of the community who speaks the same language as the children at the orphanage to make regular visits to your class. Together, translate students' letters to children at the orphanage into their language. Translate a favorite folktale or fairy tale (told in students' words) into that language and send an illustrated copy to the orphanage.

Social Studies: Brainstorm a list of needs that are common to people around the world. Have students discuss how those needs are met in their homes and communities. Discuss possible reasons for families and communities having difficulty meeting those needs.

Math: Have students keep journals of their weekly food intake. Using newspaper grocery store inserts and general knowledge, have them calculate the approximate cost of their food each week, then figure the cost of feeding a child for one week based on an average of all the students' calculations.

Modification idea from Brenda Sohlich's 1988–89 second-grade students at St. Philip Elementary in Battle Creek, Michigan—Kids Care Contest merit winner.

Books for the World

Project Goal
To share information about the U.S. with students in other countries.

Project Summary
Roxanne Aery's 1990–91 third-grade class at Perth Elementary School in Amsterdam, New York, researched eight topics about their country and used the information to write a big book about the United States. They shared copies of the book with students in several other countries and donated a copy to their school library.

Citizenship Goal
To encourage understanding and friendship among children around the world in order to promote a more friendly, cooperative world for all.

Preparation
Before setting out to gather research, agree as a class on the topics to be included in the book. First, have students imagine they are going to move to another country. What would they be curious about? Possibilities include food, school, dress, children's literature, sports, entertainment, music, art, language, government, transportation, holidays, symbols, and landmarks. List research topics and assign teams of students to each.

Procedure
1. Provide students with class time for gathering information. Encourage them to use a variety of resources, including those found in the library and computer software if available. Consider people as resources, too. For example, your librarian might be able to tell students what the ten most popular children's books were this year. Interview the physical education teacher about sports. Survey students about American kids' favorite foods, music, and clothes.
2. Have each group present its research to the class. Together, brainstorm ways to present each topic. For example, students working on a chapter about food might want to present a list of students' top-ten favorite foods, give recipes for some of those foods, and write about where the ingredients for those foods come from.
3. Create polished, final versions of each chapter—keep big-book software in mind if your students have access to a computer and printer. *Clifford's Big Book Publisher* (Scholastic) and *BIG and Little/Muppet Slate* (Sunburst) are two programs students can use to create big books.
4. Add additional pages, such as a title page, an introduction with a class photo, a world map locating your country, and a U.S. map locating your city and state.

5. Make a copy for each country you will be sharing your book with. Have students illustrate all copies and send them off.

Modification

Create a multicultural book—one that represents kids and languages around the world. Instead of sending a separate copy to a school or class in each different country, route one copy to schools in various countries. Include blank pages in each chapter for schools or classes in different countries to add their own information and illustrations.

Each time the book is returned to you, make copies of the new pages (in case the book is ever lost in the mail) and send the book to a school/class in the next country on your list. Continue until you have included as many countries as desired. Send a copy of the finished book to each of the participants.

Extension Activities

Social Studies: Help other children learn the basics of good citizenship by helping them understand their own country. Take your book on tour—right in your own school. Read it to younger children and lend it to older children.

Language Arts: Promote understanding among students of different countries and cultures by joining a pen-pal program (see Resources). Exchange information about student interests, school, holidays, after-school activities, hopes for the future, local geography, and so on with a class in another country. Keep copies of letters you send and receive in a scrap book, notebook, or bound blank-page book.

Care Packages

Project Goals
To send care packages and letters to soldiers serving our country; to become aware of what freedom is; to study factors that contribute to conflicts; to develop a sense of patriotism and school pride.

Project Summary
Every two weeks, Jennifer Thomas's 1990–91 fifth graders at Cotton Indian Elementary in Stockbridge, Georgia, sent boxes of supplies to soldiers in the Middle East. They involved the whole school in getting local businesses to donate supplies and designed and sold T-shirts to raise money for additional supplies. They also organized a countywide cookie drive and sent more than 100,000 cookies to the soldiers. During the course of their project, students formed pen-pal relationships with many of the soldiers. This class won a Kids Care Contest merit award for its project.

Preparation
Contact your local army, navy, airforce or marines office (see Resources) to find out where American military personnel are stationed. Invite someone from these offices to come in to talk to your class about the different branches of the U.S. military, responsibilities of service men and women while on duty, and their day-to-day activities. Make arrangements for your students to adopt a service man or woman as a pen pal. Try to arrange for your students' letters and packages to be sent aboard military ships or planes.

Procedure
1. Have students write letters to their military pen pal, exchanging information about themselves, their families, and their geographic location. Students may want to ask their pen pal if there is anything they would like sent to them.
2. After students have a list of items that their military pen pal would like, they can begin collecting the items. Students can ask other students, family members, community members, and local businesses to make donations (either money to buy the supplies, or the actual items that service men or women have requested).
3. Design and sell T-shirts to raise money to buy additional supplies.
4. Organize a cookie drive. Make posters asking community members to drop off cookies to your school on a particular day.
5. Once all the supplies are collected, box them (protect cookies by packing them with popcorn), add personal notes or drawings, and ship.

Modification
Contact your local veterans' organizations to obtain a list of veterans in your community. Have students prepare a list of questions to ask

veterans, so they can find out more about them and their experiences. Prepare a special play or presentation for the veterans.

Extension Activities

Social Studies: Have students find out more about the state or country that their military pen pal is stationed in. Looking at a map, have students determine how they would get from where they are to where their pen pal is stationed. How many states or countries would they pass through? What would be the best mode of transportation? If your students' pen pal is traveling, have them use yarn to track their pen pal's voyage on a map.

Math: Using a scale of miles, have students figure out how many miles it is from where they are located to where their military pen pal is stationed. If the currency where their pen pal is located is different, have students figure out the exchange rate.

Language Arts: Have students design their own postcards to send to their pen pal. On the postcard they should write something about their com-munity or state. Or, instead of postcards, students can write travel brochures of their community to familiarize their pen pal with where they live.

Modification idea from Rochelle Peters's sixth-grade students at North Elementary School in Goodland, Kansas—1989–90 Kids Care Contest merit winners.

Children to Children

Project Goal
To support immigrants on their arrival to the U.S.

Project Summary
Sheila Zachter's 1989–90 third-grade students at the Elm Park School in Staten Island, New York, read about Russian immigrants, including children, who were arriving in New York City. This class held book and toy drives, made welcome posters, and prepared a performance of patriotic songs. They welcomed the children with a presentation of their gifts and songs.

Citizenship Goals
To be aware of the reasons people leave their home countries to make their homes in other countries; to learn that living in a democratic society carries responsibilities as well as rights.

Preparation
Contact your local immigration agency or a social or family service agency for information on helping new immigrants. Depending on the time and place, you may or may not find a group of immigrants moving into your area. If not, consider helping a group settling in another part of your state or even in another part of the country.

Procedure
1. Organize used toy and book drives. Create a campaign to raise schoolwide awareness of the project. Design posters and fliers and make P.A. announcements inviting students and staff to participate. Specify, if possible, the age range of the children who will be receiving the gifts, the kinds of toys and books you're looking for, and details about when and where to bring the donations.
2. As toys and books arrive, work together to clean, repair, and sort them.
3. Draw colorful welcome signs or cards for each immigrant child.
4. Prepare songs to perform for your new friends. Include songs about your country such as "America the Beautiful" and "This Land is Your Land."
5. Put your gifts together and arrange to present them to your new friends. If you're unable to go in person, make an audio- or videotape of your song performance, pack that up with the other gifts, and either mail the box or find a volunteer to deliver it to a local organization that helps immigrants resettle or a temporary home for new immigrants.

Paper Cranes for Peace

Project Goal
To extend a gesture of sympathy and friendship to the people of Japan and to remind world leaders to strive for a peaceful world.

Project Summary
Librarian Marianne Murray and 1988–89 fourth- and fifth-grade students at Burling School, Carlson School, and Longfellow School in Pennsauken, New Jersey, read *Sadako and the Thousand Paper Cranes* by Eleanor Coerr (Putnam, 1977), the story of a twelve-year-old child who died as a result of radiation from the bombing of Hiroshima. Sadako Sasaki thought that if she could fold 1,000 origami paper cranes, a miracle would happen and she would get well. She made 644 before she died. As a gesture of sympathy and peace, Murray's students folded the remaining 356 paper cranes and sent them to the Hiroshima Peace Memorial Hall in Japan. They took their message of peace worldwide by writing letters and sending paper cranes to world leaders as a reminder of the horrors of war and a symbol of hope for a peaceful world. They won a Kids Care Contest grand prize for their project.

Citizenship Goal
To learn that everyone can be part of the effort for world peace.

Preparation
Begin by discussing the bombing of Hiroshima in 1945. Read about the rebuilding of the city, including the Peace Park erected after the war, and the Children's Peace Monument, erected in memory of Sadako Sasaki. Use library resources, including children's literature such as *Hiroshima No Pika* by Toshi Maruki (Lothrup, 1982) and *Sadako and the Thousand Paper Cranes* (see Project Summary). Talk about using symbols, such as a paper crane, to promote a cause.

Procedure
1. Consult books on origami for directions on folding paper cranes.
2. Create a paper crane corner in your classroom:
- make signs that illustrate the steps of folding an origami paper crane;
- decorate a box to hold scrap paper for making the cranes;
- decorate a second box for holding completed cranes; and
- create a pictograph to record your progress.

3. Fold the first batch of paper cranes together to familiarize students with the process. Thereafter, you may wish to let students make cranes as they have time, or set aside a special time for this activity during the day, such as before morning announcements or after lunch.
4. As the second box fills up, count the cranes and record progress on the pictograph. Empty the box periodically to make room for more cranes, storing finished cranes in a closet or other space where they will

not be crushed or create a fire hazard.

5. When you have reached your goal, pack your cranes for mailing and send them to the Hiroshima Peace Memorial Hall to be offered to the Children's Peace Monument (see Resources).

6. Over the course of this project, have students write to world leaders, expressing their concerns for a peaceful world and enclose an origami paper crane in each letter as a symbol of students' concerns and hopes. Try to write to at least one world leader every month.

Modification

Spread the message of peace in your own school by creating a peace center in your library. Include:
- children's books that express peaceful themes (including those about friendship and conflict resolution);
- books about Hiroshima and other war-related tragedies;
- biographies about leaders for peace (such as Martin Luther King and Ghandi);
- student reports, stories, and drawings about working for world peace;
- samples of symbols of peace (such as the origami paper crane, the peace sign, and the dove and olive branch);
- newsclippings about peace efforts;
- audiotapes of songs about peace (such as Cat Steven's "Peace Train" and John Lennon's "Give Peace a Chance");
- graphs and charts summarizing the effects of past wars;
- names and addresses of world leaders to whom students can write in support of world peace.

Extension Activities

Language Arts: Learn the word for peace in other languages by consulting foreign language dictionaries, asking students from other countries in their school, or writing ambassadors of other countries. Put the words together to make a peace banner. Hang it in the library or lobby.

Art: Have students design their own symbols for peace. Challenge students to combine elements from different symbols to create world flags for peace.

Dramatic Arts: Devise a plan to keep the peace in your own school. Have students role play situations that often result in conflicts, such as: You're working on an art project and you want the markers someone else is using. But he says he needs them all. Or, you're on the playground and you get hit with a ball. You think someone hit you on purpose. Discuss alternatives to the less than peaceful solutions.

Science/Social Studies: Whooping cranes are one of the rarest birds in North America. Now they're protected by international law. Using research, have students devise methods for bringing them back. Next, have them write an environmental law that would prevent species not currently endangered from becoming so due to destruction of their habitat.

Trees for Ireland

Project Goal
To help reforest Ireland.

Project Summary
Mary Bushey's 1990–91 first-grade students at the International School of Minnesota in Eden Prairie, Minnesota, learned that Ireland is the least forested country in Europe. They raised money through a penny-collecting campaign to have three trees planted in Ireland as part of the Irish American Cultural Institute's ongoing effort to restore Ireland's woodlands.

Citizenship Goals
To recognize the world as a larger community and to learn that people working together can effect change even as far away as another country.

Preparation
Begin by learning about Ireland—its land, people, culture, customs, and needs. Contact the Irish American Cultural Institute for more information about the Trees for Ireland reforestation program (see Resources).

Procedure
1. Set a class goal—at $25 each, how many trees do you want to donate to Ireland?
2. Plan your penny-saving campaign. Who will participate—your class, your grade, the entire school? Design containers to hold the pennies, for example half-gallon milk cartons or liter soda bottles (cut tops off) decorated to look like trees. If you invite other classes to participate in the fund-raiser, sponsor a contest for the most creative container.
3. Arrange the details of penny collection—how often and by whom will containers be emptied? Does the main office have a safe place for storing the pennies until they are rolled and brought to a bank?
4. Plan an event to kick off your fund-raising campaign. You might invite a bagpipe player to share traditional music, a representative from a nearby Irish American Cultural Institute (or someone else who is involved in Irish studies) to answer questions, or a storyteller to share Irish folktales.
5. Every so often, plan penny rolling into your day. Have students work in teams to count out piles of 50 and roll them. Keep a pictograph of your progress.
6. As you near your goal, begin researching individual counties of Ireland. Take a class vote on where you would like the trees planted. Make a map of Ireland and its counties and place pictures of trees where your donations will grow.

Modification

You may want to take a class vote to decide on your own fund-raising campaign. Possibilities include an Irish fair celebrating the customs, foods, and art of Ireland or a themed school shop where you sell items related to your project, such as green tree bookmarks, green pencils, notecards in the shape of the Ireland, tree-shaped cookies, or mini Irish soda breads.

Extension Activities

Language Arts: Bring Ireland into your classroom with folktales. For starters try *Fin M'Coul: The Giant of Knockmany Hill*, retold by Tomie dePaola (Holiday, 1981); *Daniel O'Rourke: An Irish Tale* by Gerald McDermott (Viking, 1986); *Guleesh and the King of France's Daughter* by Neil Philip (Putnam, 1986); and *A Treasury of Irish Folklore* edited by Padraic Colum (Crown, 1969).

Math: Make estimation part of your penny-collection campaign. Challenge students to estimate the number of pennies in the first container collected. Next have them estimate how many containers of pennies it will take to reach your goal. Record students' estimates periodically and allow revisions to the original figures as students develop their estimation skills.

Social Studies: Turn a bulletin board into a world map keyed to show forestation in countries around the world. Which countries are most heavily forested? Least? Provide special designation for countries where rainforests are being leveled-cut for lumber, agriculture, and cattle farming.

Science: Ireland is being reforested with a diversity of species including sitka spruce, lodgepole pine, oak, birch, and ash. Have students compare forests in Ireland with forests here. How are they alike? How are they different?

RESOURCES

The following are just some of the organizations, books, and government offices that can help you accomplish your project goals. Learn about additional resources by checking with your school and local libraries.

GLOBAL AWARENESS

World Vision
919 W. Huntington Dr.
Monrovia, CA 91016
(800)423-4200
To sponsor a child.

Children International
P.O. Box 419055
Kansas City, MO 64141
(800)888-3089
To sponsor a child.

United Nations Children's Fund (UNICEF)
Three United Nations Plaza
New York, NY 10017
(212)326-7000
To assist children worldwide in getting food, health care, and education.

Bibliotecas Betsy McWilliams Inc.
2899 Glenmore Rd.
Shaker Heights, OH 44122
(216)751-4349
To provide books and establish libraries in orhanages of Central American countries.

United Service Organizations
World Headquarters
601 Indiana Ave., NW
Washington, DC 20004
(202)783-8121
To correspond with service men and women.

Peace Corps Partnership Program
1990 K St., NW
Washington, DC 20526
(800)424-8580
To aid schools overseas in need of basic equipment and materials.

Evangelical Association for the Promotion of Education
P.O. Box 238
St. Davids, PA 19087
(215)341-1722
To aid schools in need of basic equipment and supplies.

International Pen Friends
P.O. Box 290065
Brooklyn, NY 11229-0001
(718)769-1785
To connect with pen friends in more than 150 countries, including the USSR (send SASE for information).

Hiroshima Peace Memorial Hall
6-34 Kokutaiji-machi 1-chome
Naka-ku, Hiroshima 730-91 Japan
Paper cranes for peace project.

Trees for Ireland
Irish American Cultural Institute
University of St. Thomas (Mail #5026)
2115 Summit Ave.
St. Paul, MN 55105
(800)232-ERIN
To reforest Ireland.

ENVIRONMENTAL/ ANIMAL ISSUES

International Wildlife Coalition
Whale Adoption Project
P.O. Box 388
634 N. Falmouth Hwy.
North Falmouth, MA 02556
(508)564-9980
To protect wildife and wildlife habitats.

Earth Island Institute
300 Broadway, Suite 28
San Franscisco, CA 94133-3312
(415)788-3666
For educational resources on ecological issues, including dolphins and sea turtles.

Whale and Dolphin Conservation Society
Inquiries Dept.
191 Weston Rd.
Lincoln, MA 01773
(617)259-0423
To adopt a whale or to receive *Whales and Dolphins of the World*, a bulletin written especially for kids (send request on school letterhead).

Save the Manatee Club
500 N. Maitland Ave., Suite 210
Maitland, FL 32751
(800)432-JOIN
To adopt a manatee.

The North American Bluebird Society
Box 6295
Silver Spring, MD 20906
(301)384-2798
For information on bluebirds, including bluebird nest plans (send $1 and business-sized SASE).

Project Wind Seine
Cape May Bird Observatory
P.O. Box 3
Cape May Point, NJ 08212
(609)884-2736
To adopt a migrating bird.

African Wildlife Foundation
1717 Massachusetts Ave., NW
Washington, DC 20036
(800)344-TUSK
For information on endangered elephants and rhinoceroses.

World Wildlife Fund
Public Programs Dept.
1250 24th St., NW
Washington, DC 20037
(202)293-4800
For information on tropical rainforests and wildlife protection programs.

Friends of the Sea Lion
Marine Mammal Center
20612 Laguna Canyon Rd.
Laguna Beach, CA 92651
(714)494-3050
To rehabilitate sick and injured seals and sea lions.

Children's Rainforest
P.O. Box 936
Lewiston, ME 04240
(207)784-1069
To save the Costa Rican rainforest.

Acid Rain Foundation
1410 Varsity Dr.

Raleigh, NC 27606
(919)828-9443
For educational materials, grades K–12.

U.S. Field and Wildlife Service
Department of the Interior
18th and C St., NW
Washington, DC 20240
(202) 208-5634
For information on endangered species.

Environmental Defense Fund
257 Park Ave. South
New York, NY 10010
(800)225-5333
For information on recycling.

Renew America
1400 16th St., NW, Suite 710
Washington, DC 20036
(202) 232-2252
A clearinghouse of more than 1200 environmental projects, many of them by kids.

U.S. Environmental Protection Agency
Public Information Center
401 M. St., SW
Washington, DC 20460
(202) 475-7751
For a directory of environmental education materials for grades K–6.

SOCIAL ACTION, COMMUNITY AWARENESS, PEOPLE PARTNERSHIPS
Habitat for Humanity, International
121 Habitat St.
Americus, GA 31709
(912)924-6935
To help build homes for homeless and disabled people.

American Institute of Architects
1735 New York Ave., NW
Washington, DC 20006
(202)626-7300
For information on architecture education programs with elementary schools.

Educators for Social Responsibility
23 Garden St.
Cambridge, MA 02138
(617)492-1764
For curriculum material for K–adult on nuclear education issues.

The Good Bears of the World
P.O. Box 8236
Honolulu, HI 96815
(808)942-0200
To provide teddy bears as comfort for children in traumatic situations.

Bicycle Federation of America
1818 R St., NW
Washington, DC 20009
(202)332-6986
For information on community-based cycling programs.

Red Ribbon Headquarters
University of California
Davis, CA 95616
(916)752-2820
For anti-drug activities and information.

Ronald McDonald House
1 Kroc Dr., Campus Office Bldg.
Oak Brook, IL 60521
(708)575-7418
For information on volunteering for a Ronald McDonald House.

United Neighborhood Centers of America
1319 F St., NW; Suite 603
Washington, DC 20004
(202)393-3929
To improve the quality of life in neighborhoods by organizing new neighborhood centers.

Public Health Service
Public Affairs
Hubert H. Humphrey Bldg.
200 Independence Ave., SW
Room 725-H
Washington, DC 20201
(202)245-6678
For information on health issues, including AIDS and drug abuse.

TO WRITE GOVERNMENT OFFICIALS
The President of the United States
White House Office
1600 Pennsylvania Ave.
Washington, DC 20500
(202)456-1414

Your Congressperson
House Office Bldg.
Washington, DC 20515

Your Senator
Senate Office Building
Washington, DC 202230

BOOKS
The Kids' Guide to Social Action by Barbara Lewis (Free Spirit Publishing Inc., 1991) (800)735-7323. Everything kids need to tackle problems and make a difference.

How Green Are You? by David Bellamy (Potter, 1991). Background information, tips, and activities for making the world a better place.

Our Only Earth by Micki McKisson and Linda MacRae Campbell (Zephyr Press, 1990). A series of six books that include information and activities on air pollution, poverty, hunger, overpopulation, tropical rain forests, and endangered species.

The Encyclopedia of Associations (Gale Research, 1990). A directory of more than 22,000 clubs, associations, and organizations. Updated annually.

ENTERING THE KIDS CARE CONTEST

Scholastic News's nationwide Kids Care Contest is designed to motivate students to participate in projects that help others and to teach them the basic concepts of citizenship. The following information and entry form is provided to assist you and your students in entering the Scholastic News Kids Care Contest. Prizes are awarded at each grade level.

CHOOSING A PROJECT

Kids Care projects don't have to cost money or take extra time in your day. In fact, you just might find, as Timothy Sullivan did, that there's a project already going on in your class. His students from Concord, New Hampshire, were involved in a traffic safety project. He said "Hey, I'm already doing this—I might as well submit these (Kids Care Contest) forms."

Project ideas also grow from problems and needs kids see in their own community, such as garbage littering the playground, or elderly people in need of assistance. Other ideas come from issues that kids read or hear about in the news, such as pollution, homelessness, or disappearing rain forests. Curriculum studies are another source of project ideas. For example, a unit on endangered animals can lead to a project to help protect whales.

Or, do what Carolyn Rodgers's students from Norman, Oklahoma, did—"We wrote to the chamber of commerce and got the names, addresses, and phone numbers of all the agencies in our town. We picked about 25 and wrote letters explaining the project and asked if they had things that needed to be done that we could help with."

GETTING STARTED

Once you've chosen a project and set a goal, agree on strategies for meeting this goal. For example, if you decide to help curb litter in your school neighborhood, your goals might be to pick up litter once a week, recycle as much of the waste as possible, display posters in the area encouraging others to pitch in, and further beautify the area by using money from recycling to plant flowers in the area's public spaces.

Finally, document your progress. Photographs of your kids in action, letters from people and organizations they've helped, student essays and drawings about their project, copies of letters and fliers students sent as part of their project, and videotapes are all ways to show growth.

CONTEST RULES

1. Any citizenship project that encourages your students to help others is eligible. The project may benefit people at home, in school, or around the community. It may help people directly, as with a project teaming students with seriously ill children in a hospital, or indirectly, as with a project that involves kids in saving dolphins. Your project need not be completed to be entered.

2. A class may enter one project or several. (Each project requires a separate entry form.) Make photocopies of the entry form for yourself and for other teachers who wish to enter.

3. Include the completed form plus any additional materials that you feel illustrate the success of your students' project, such as student essays and drawings, photographs, letters from people who were helped by your students, and local news coverage of your project.

4. All materials must fit inside a 9-by-12-inch envelope and be mailed to: Kids Care Contest, Scholastic News, 730 Broadway, New York, NY 10003. Entries should be postmarked no later than December 31, of the school year you are entering.

5. Projects entered will be judged on their success in making a positive contribution to society and in teaching students basic concepts of citizenship. Creativity and originality will also be considered. The size of the project, in terms of money raised or number of people helped, is not important—the time and effort you and your kids commit to the project count most.

6. Judging will be by *Scholastic News* editors and a panel of distinguished educators. Winners will be notified by phone and announced in a spring issue of *Scholastic News*.

7. All entries become the property of Scholastic Inc. We regret that we can not return any entries. Employees of Scholastic Inc. and immediate members of their family are not eligible for prizes. Contest is void where prohibited by law.

KIDS CARE

Scholastic News
Kids Care Contest
ENTRY FORM
(PLEASE PRINT OR TYPE)

Teacher's Name_____ Grade_____

Principal's Name_____

School Name_____

School Address_____

Date_____ Telephone Number_____

CITIZENSHIP PROJECT
Briefly Describe Your Class Project (attach extra sheets if needed)

Project Goals

What We Did/Are Doing

What We Learned About Citizenship

Grand prize winning classes win the opportunity to donate prize money to the nonsectarian or nonprofit organization of their choice. Please list a designated recipient.

Name of Organization_____

Contact's Name_____

Telephone Number (____)_____

PRESS CONTACTS

Local Newspaper_____

Address_____

Local Network or Cable TV Station_____

Address_____